The Joy of Belonging

Discovering Who You Are In Christ

WOODROW KROLL

BACK TO THE BIBLE
Lincoln, Nebraska

10,000 printed to date—1996
(1160-050—10M—596)
ISBN 0-8474-1468-X

Printed in the United States of America.

Acknowledgments

The Joy of Belonging is the product of some very special people. Although the content of this book was originally part of my teaching on the *Back to the Bible* radio broadcast, a team of very capable colleagues has made it possible for those messages to become a part of this book. I want to express my appreciation to them.

Thanks to Allen Bean, my researcher and assistant, whose diligence in checking sources, rewriting copy and making helpful additions immensely improved this volume. Thanks to Rachel Derowitsch, senior editor for Back to the Bible publications, who contributed helpful corrections and editorial suggestions. Thanks to Kim Johnson, whose creativity initiated the cover design concept. Thanks also to Bob Peterson and his staff of skilled print professionals for the publication of this book. Finally, thanks to my administrative assistant, Cathy Strate, who tirelessly aids me in every facet of my radio and publication responsibilities. The joy of belonging to this team of competent and dedicated people makes my ministry even more enjoyable. Together we pray that this book will enhance your joy in discovering who you are in Christ.

Contents

Introduction

In 1995 Back to the Bible received on cassette tape the testimony of a woman whose heart and life had been touched by our ministry. Shortly after receiving Christ, Sara Risca began working at *La Biblia Dice . . .* (which means "The Bible Says . . ."), our international office in Quito, Ecuador. Of the *La Biblia Dice* staff she said, "They gave me medicine, they gave me love, and they gave me a job." In short, she was saying that our staff made her feel as if she had found a place where she belonged.

But it didn't end there. One day Sara saw a map of Jamaica on the office wall. In a broken voice she explained that she had been separated from her brother, Charles, when they were children and that he was somewhere in Kingston, Jamaica. "Do you think that *La Biblia Dice* could find my brother for me?" she asked. One of the staff responded, "All things are possible when Jesus wants to do His will."

Months went by and no news was received. Then one day a call came. It was from Back to the Bible's office in Kingston, Jamaica. They had located a Charles M. It was Sara's brother, whom she had not seen since he was nine years old! As the last living members of their family, Charles and Sara soon had a joyful reunion. They belonged together.

The testimony continued. Sara also had a son, John, whom she had not seen for 30 years. Again God provided a miracle. She not only found her son but also discovered he was married and the father of two children, making her a grandmother. "At last I have somebody who is my own!" Sara said.

What joy there is in belonging, to know that we are not alone but are surrounded by those who care, to be part of a family.

We all want to belong. Today adolescent boys sport earrings, wear pants down around their thighs and—what I used to fuss about as a boy—have haircuts that look like mine did when my father put a bowl on my head and shaved around it. Boys dress this way not to appear different but to belong. Some college freshmen endure hazing and humiliation in order to belong to a fraternity or sorority. Belonging means you are part of something. It means there are people who value you as "part of them."

The joy of belonging also is experienced when one becomes a Christian. This belonging, however, is not based on what we wear or how we look. It stems solely from what Christ did for us at Calvary's cross. Paul told the Christians at Colosse, "He [Christ] has delivered us from the power of darkness and translated us into the kingdom of the Son of His love" (Col. 1:13). We were once lost and far from God, but now, through Christ, we have come home where we belong. John W. Peterson wrote,

A pilgrim was I, and a-wan-d'ring,
In the cold night of sin I did roam,

When Jesus the kind Shepherd found me,

And now I am on my way home.[1]

Home. What a heartwarming word. For most people it is a reminder of how wonderful it is to belong!

Many organizations offer you the opportunity to join them. For a fee you can belong to a health spa, a service organization or a social club. Pay the money and you, too, can belong. God, however, offers us the opportunity to belong to His family with no fees attached.

Some people find this difficult to believe. Bible teacher G. Campbell Morgan told of a coal miner who said to him, "I would give anything to believe that God would forgive my sins, but I can't believe that all I have to do is ask Him. It's too cheap."

Morgan wanted to help the man understand, so he asked, "My friend, have you been working today?"

"Yes, I was down in the mine," the man replied.

"How did you get out?" Mr. Morgan asked. "Did you pay?"

"Of course not," the miner said. "I just got into a cage and was pulled to the top."

"Weren't you afraid to entrust yourself to that cage? Wasn't it too cheap?" Morgan asked.

"Oh, no," the man said, "it was cheap for me, but it cost the company a lot of money to sink the shaft."

Suddenly the truth struck the miner. To become a part

of God's family would cost him nothing, but it cost God dearly. He had paid an expensive price—His Son—to provide salvation for us.

God's offer to belong is not only free, it's eternal. When we become a part of God's family, we belong forever. Jesus said, "My Father, who has given them to Me, is greater than all; and no one is able to snatch them out of My Father's hand" (John 10:29).

In contrast, man's security is flimsy. Aldrich Ames worked for the Central Intelligence Agency—and for the KGB. As a double agent he revealed the secret identity of more than 100 other agents and prospective agents. He provided reams of highly classified information to the Russian government. According to CIA director John Deutch, this breach of security "will take years and years to recover from."[2] Almost everyone who belonged to the CIA was placed in danger.

Our membership in God's family, however, places us in the strong arms of the Lord, where we are far more secure than anyone in the CIA. We belong, but it's no secret. It's something to talk about, sing about, enjoy to the fullest of our being.

It's understandable, then, why I call this the "joy" of belonging. As we explore what it means to belong to Christ, I pray that you may discover the joy of belonging and that your joy may increase more than ever before.

[1] John W. Peterson, "Surely Goodness and Mercy," Singspiration, Inc., 1958 and 1965.

[2] Donald M. Rothberg, "Spy in CIA gave away 100 agents," *Lincoln Journal Star*, November 1, 1995, p. A-1.

Chapter 1

Belonging: The Basis for Significance

Presidents do it; fathers do it; writers do it; teens do it; business people do it; even preachers do it. What do they do? They attempt to find significance.

Wherever we live, whatever we do for a living, we are constantly searching for significance. Almost everything we do is designed to establish that we are significant people. Presidents are concerned that future generations will view their presidency as significant. Writers seek to create that great American novel so future readers will recognize their literary significance. Fathers want to be remembered by their children as having a significant and positive influence on their lives. Business leaders want to make their mark as movers and shakers, significant barons in the business community. Even preachers desire to significantly impact those who sit under their ministry.

Webster defines significance as "the quality of having meaning; having or likely to have an influence on others." Within each of us is a drive to find meaning in our existence. To remove a person's significance—his sense of meaning in life—is to condemn him to despair.

In his book *Kingdoms in Conflict*, Charles Colson tells

of a concentration camp in Hungary where hundreds of Jewish prisoners lived on little food in disease-infested barracks. They were forced to do backbreaking factory work until the camp was bombed by Allied planes. With the factory destroyed there was no more work to do. Their Nazi captors, however, decided to keep the prisoners busy by moving a large pile of sand to the far end of the camp. When the prisoners had finished, the Nazis ordered them to haul it back to the other end of the camp. This happened day after day with no apparent reason. Finally, one old man began crying uncontrollably; the guards hauled him away. Another began to scream until he was beaten into silence. Dozens of prisoners went mad and ran from their work, only to be shot by the guards or electrocuted by the fence that surrounded the compound. What hardship and deprivation were unable to do, a life without meaning accomplished.[1]

Rabbi Harold Kushner observes, "The need for meaning is not a biological need (like food or air). Neither is it a psychological need like acceptance and self-esteem. It is a religious need."[2] Only God can meet that need, and He does so through our relationship with Him. All of us were made to relate to God intimately, to experience a depth of belonging that knows no barriers. God created us with a built-in significance.

That all people were originally significant is reflected in the account of man's creation in the Book of Genesis. We see our significance in:

The order of man's creation

In the secular world, last place is highly undesirable. If you don't win a race, by all means make sure you at least don't come in last. Some of us remember the embarrassment of being the last one chosen for a game when we were children. Last! Who wants to be last? But don't think last is always least. Sometimes last is the best position.

In God's creation man was last, but it was not a position of shame; it was a place of honor. Our creation was not an afterthought; it was the capstone, the crown of God's creative efforts. God began by creating light and separating it from darkness (Gen. 1:3-5). Following this He created the dry land, the plants and the animals. His world was the most beautiful setting you could ever imagine, but it lacked one thing—a jewel. The triune Godhead said, "Let Us make man in Our image" (v. 26). All that He had created was preparatory to this one glorious moment, the moment when God would put the finishing touch on His creation— and man became a living being. What the dot is to the "i" and the cross stroke is to the "t," you and I are in God's creation. We are the finishing touch on creation.

A person's final touches are usually the most important. They are those things that, if left undone, would spoil all the previous work. The final strokes of a brush on a work of art, the final decorations on a birthday cake, that last touch of the hair to make it perfect, are all evidence of a guiding force that genuinely cares about the product or the result. The fact that God reserved man's creation to the end should indicate to us just how important this final touch was to Him. You were created significant.

The method of man's creation

For thousands of years, glass makers have relied on five techniques for making glass products. They have cast it (poured molten glass into a mold and allowed it to solidify); pressed it (used a plunger to press it into a mold); drawn it (simply taken it directly from the furnace); rolled it (poured that glass onto a flat surface and smoothed it with a roller); and blown it. In this last method, the blower (called a gaffer) takes a four-foot blowpipe and gathers a lump of molten glass on the end. Using paddles and his own breath, he enlarges, shapes and decorates it. By skillful manipulation, he creates some of the most beautiful and artistic objects the world has ever seen.

It is with the utmost respect and awe that I say God, too, is a gaffer. But instead of glass, God blew the breath of life into a lump of clay and it "became a living being" (Gen. 2:7). For everything else God spoke and it came into existence. That in itself is a miracle. But man was a special miracle. A part of God, His breath, was instilled into this lifeless lump to make it a living creature. God gave us significance by the unique method in which He created us.

Man shares this uniqueness with only one other thing— the Word of God. Second Timothy 3:16 says, "All Scripture is given by inspiration of God, and is profitable for doctrine, for reproof, for correction, for instruction in righteousness." The word translated as "inspiration" literally means "God-breathed." It is exhaled, arising from the being of God. Anything that is God-breathed is special and is designed to speak to others about Him. Just as there is no other book like the Bible, there is no other creation like man. That in itself is significant, as we are significant.

The pattern of man's creation

But there's much more to the significance of our creation. Man was created in God's image. When God said, "Let Us make man in Our image, according to Our likeness," He wasn't speaking to the angels. If He were, we would have been fashioned after both God and the angels, an angelic pattern of God. We humans are not part-divine and part-angelic. God was referring to His Triune Self when He said, "Let Us make . . ." We are patterned totally after God's image.

Does this mean that God has two hands, two feet, two eyes, etc., as we do? Not at all. The Scriptures sometimes refer to the "hand of God" (15 times in the NKJV) or the "eyes of the Lord" (20 times), but that is not meant to imply God has a body like we do. This literary technique is called anthropomorphizing, "to attribute human form to things not human." Scripture clearly teaches that God is Spirit (John 4:24), but many traits are expressed in human terms to give us a better understanding as we seek to relate to Him.

Being created in the image of God is far more important than just human appearance. We share with God many spiritual qualities, such as:

Self-consciousness. God gave man the ability to be aware of himself. We are able to think about ourselves in terms of who we are and, most important, why we exist. It is this ability to think about ourselves and be conscious of our failures that enables us to become aware of our need for a Savior.

Satan does his best to prevent us from giving ourselves much serious consideration. In his delightful book *The Screwtape Letters*, C. S. Lewis depicts a senior demon, named Screwtape, sharing advice with his nephew, Wormwood, on how to keep us from considering ourselves or our need for God. Screwtape once had influence over an atheist who began to think about spiritual topics. Immediately Screwtape turned the man's thoughts to lunch. When the man went out for lunch, "the battle was won. I showed him a newsboy shouting the midday paper, and a No. 73 bus going past. . . . Whatever odd ideas might come into a man's head when he was shut up alone with his books, a healthy dose of 'real life' [by which he meant the bus and the newsboy] was enough to show him that all 'that sort of thing' just couldn't be true."[3]

The fact that you have any ability at all to think of yourself and how you relate to the deeper meaning of life is unique to human beings. No other animal ever asks itself, "Who am I?" Only man has that special gift. That makes us significant in God's creation.

Speech. Animals can make noise. Anyone who has heard two cats yowling late at night in the alley knows that. Sometimes they even seem to be able to talk to us. Linda and I have a Saint Bernard named Brienz. There are times when I think that dog knows everything we say to her. Mention "walk" and she gets her leash. Say "ride" and she's at the door of the garage. But Brienz can't have a meaningful chat with me. None of God's earthly creation can carry on abstract, extended conversations like man can.

It is estimated that the average person spends one-fifth of his or her life talking. Perhaps that explains why the two older ladies on their first airplane flight were concerned. They stopped the flight attendant and asked her to convey a message to the pilot. "Certainly," the attendant replied. "What would you like for me to tell him?" "Please tell him," one of the ladies said, "not to fly faster than the speed of sound. We want to talk." Talking is a part of our lives every day. Animals communicate as well. We are all amazed at the ability of porpoises and whales to communicate. But it would be quite a stretch to say that they talk. Man is unique in God's creation.

Moral discernment. This is the innate ability to detect right from wrong. Adam knew when he partook of the fruit of the tree of the knowledge of good and evil that he was disobeying. This knowledge of wrong plus the guilt and fear it creates caused him to flee and hide from the presence of God (Gen. 3:8). When God found him, Adam had to admit, "I heard Your voice in the garden, and I was afraid because I was naked; and I hid myself" (v. 10). Man knows when he has done something wrong. As Mark Twain used to say, "Man is the only creature that blushes, or needs to."

But don't animals know when they have done wrong? My Saint Bernard certainly does. She wants to please us so much, and when she does something that displeases us her jowls droop and her eyes look so sad. She has a sense that she has done wrong, but she doesn't have a moral code by which to judge what she did wrong. She knows it is wrong to jump into my bed when I get out in the morning, but only because we have told her it is wrong. She doesn't know that intuitively. She has no moral discernment like you and I have. That's just one more significance given to us by our Creator.

Sovereignty. God invested His sovereignty over the earth to man. He told Adam and Eve to "be fruitful and multiply; fill the earth and subdue it; have dominion over the fish of the sea, over the birds of the air, and over every living thing that moves on the earth. . . . See, I have given you every herb that yields seed which is on the face of all the earth, and every tree whose fruit yields seed; to you it shall be for food" (Gen. 1:28–29). Man was to take control of earth. He was to have dominion over all creation.

Today our sovereignty is different from God's because our morality has been tainted by sin. We rule over the earth, but our dark hearts cause us to pollute the environment and the earth over which we are to have dominion. We do not worship the earth, but we are God's caretakers of it, and all people who are morally in tune with the heart of God will respect the earth while we subdue it. Still, we are sovereign, and no other creature on God's green earth is. That's how significant God created us.

The likeness of man's creation

Even the likeness of God in our creation gives us significance. We are made in the likeness of God with more than spiritual qualities. Our composition resembles that of God. A plant is made as a plant; a tree is as a tree. There is a physical presence and life, but there is no life-giving spirit. God did not breathe into trees the breath of life. They are alive, but not alive with God's spirit.

Man, however, is different. We are even different from other animals. The horse has a body and a soul (the breath of life, that which makes it animate). It is a mobile, living creature. But it has no God-spirit. You and I are quite different. As God is a triune creature, we also are triune creations. As God is composed of Father, Son and Holy Spirit (yet one God), so man is composed of body, soul and spirit (yet one person). If man had only a body, he would be like a tree. If he had but body and soul, he would be like an animal. But since he has body, soul and spirit, man is like God. Doesn't that give us significance in creation?

The purpose of man's creation

Furthermore, God immediately gave man a purpose. As part of God's creation, he was to fulfill certain responsibilities. Genesis 2:15 says, "Then the LORD God took the man and put him in the garden of Eden to tend and keep it." That sounds like work, and this was before the Fall. Adam also was responsible for naming the animals. Verse 19 says, "Out of the ground the LORD God formed every beast of the field and every bird of the air, and brought them to

Adam to see what he would call them. And whatever Adam called each living creature, that was its name." The animals did not name themselves; the plants did not till themselves. Man had purpose right from the beginning that the rest of God's creation did not have.

The greatest purpose God gave man, however, was to have fellowship with Him. Work in and of itself soon grows meaningless unless it is done in the context of a relationship. When what we do relates to someone we care deeply about, the labor becomes love. It's not work at all; it's simply activity that relates us to others. Someone has said that drudgery is work with the heart taken out. Nothing makes work less meaningful than having no one to relate it to.

Originally man's life and work were meaningful; they had significance because of his relationship with his Creator. Genesis 3:8 says, "And they heard the sound of the LORD God walking in the garden in the cool of the day." The verse implies that God did this regularly. Each day He spent time with Adam and Eve simply communing in a loving relationship.

No other creature had such a wonderful privilege. To walk with God, to share their innermost thoughts, to fellowship with One who understood them completely, to relate with a Person who loved them beyond their ability to understand, who accepted them as they were—these were the blessings that made life significant for Adam and Eve. The sun rose, the flowers bloomed, the birds sang because the One who created them knew they would find it pleasurable and add to their joy in relating to Him. The wonders of all this exceed our imaginations.

Are you significant? In God's eyes you are His most important creation. You are more special than the angels. You have an importance that defies description. If you are not feeling significant today, don't blame God. He created you with enough significance to last a lifetime. From the first days of Adam and Eve in Eden's Garden, people have been of the highest significance to God. You are the "apple of His eye" (Deut. 32:10; Ps. 17:8). You can experience the joy of belonging because you started out with mind-boggling significance. You were born significant.

---

[1] Charles Colson, *Kingdoms in Conflict* (Grand Rapids, Mich.: William Morrow/Zondervan Publishing House, 1987), pp. 68-69.

[2] Harold Kushner, *When All You've Ever Wanted Isn't Enough* (New York: Summit, 1986), p. 29.

[3] C. S. Lewis, *The Screwtape Letters* (New York: The Macmillan Company, 1961), p. 9.

Chapter 2

Belonging: The Casualty of Rebellion

Independence! For many of us the word triggers memories of firework displays, family gatherings and ice cream on a hot July day. Yet for God the word triggers sadness. The very thing so many people seek is a source of grief for Him.

God did not create us to be independent. Surprised? Don't be. We were never made to fully function apart from Him. It's not that we can't muddle through life without Him—billions of people have done it. But without a dependence on God, we are incomplete.

Dependency is not an abnormality. God created us specifically for a dependent relationship. In fact, our sense of significance flows out of this dependency. David Needham declares, "For a human to be truly alive—by our Creator's definition—is to live as an extension of God's own life."[1] As the blossom is an extension of the flower, as the leaf is an extension of the branch, so man is an extension of His Creator. Human beings draw their meaning and significance from their connection to God. Independence interrupts that connection and destroys our significance.

Jesus demonstrated this dependency in His life on earth. He was the only perfect man who ever lived, yet He said, "Do you not believe that I am in the Father, and the Father in Me? The words that I speak to you I do not speak on My own authority; but the Father who dwells in Me does the works" (John 14:10). Another time He said, "I have many things to say and to judge concerning you, but He who sent Me is true; and I speak to the world those things which I heard from Him" (John 8:26). Those listening to Him did not understand that He spoke about the Father, so Jesus said, "When you lift up the Son of Man, then you will know that I am He, and that I do nothing of Myself; but as My Father taught Me, I speak these things" (v. 28).

A life of dependence on God is the secret to our significance. Yet Adam and Eve's rebellion against God, their demand to be independent of His restrictions, meant a tragic loss of significance for them and all their descendants.

Satan's loss of significance

Ezekiel 28 records God's pronouncement of judgment on the prince of Tyre. Verse 2 says, "Son of man, say to the prince of Tyre, 'Thus says the Lord GOD: "Because your heart is lifted up, and you say, 'I am a god, I sit in the seat of gods, in the midst of the seas,' yet you are a man, and not a god, though you set your heart as the heart of a god.""

This is not the first time human rulers have aspired to the position of deity. In the early days of Egypt, the Pharaohs claimed to be incarnate gods on earth—especially the falcon god Horus of Upper Egypt. Later they devalued their claims and asserted they were merely the son of a god (Ra, the sun god). Beginning with Octavian (the adopted heir of Julius Caesar), the Roman senate gave its ruler the title "Augustus," meaning "the revered one." It carried the idea of worship. Although Octavian did not encourage emperor worship, it became a fact of life later in the Roman Empire. The Emperor Caligula even had temples built to himself and sacrifices offered.

But Tyre was not Rome or Egypt. So far as we know, Tyre never had a king. Therefore, when God changes the focus of His attention to the "King of Tyre" (Ezek. 28:11-19), many commentators suggest He is no longer addressing a human being but the spiritual power behind the throne—Satan. Satan was one of God's most powerful and beautiful creations. God's description of Satan before his rebellion is graphic:

> You were the seal of perfection, full of wisdom and perfect in beauty. You were in Eden, the garden of God; every precious stone was your covering: the sardius, topaz, and diamond, beryl, onyx, and jasper, sapphire, turquoise, and emerald with gold. The workmanship of your timbrels and pipes was prepared for you on the day you were created. You were the anointed cherub who covers; I established you; you were on the holy mountain of God; you walked back and forth in the midst of fiery stones. You were perfect in your ways from the day you were created (vv. 12–15).

In his book *The Invisible War*, Donald Grey Barnhouse suggests that Satan was above all the other angels. He was the funnel through which all the rest of creation channeled their worship to God.[2]

But such power and beauty were evidently more than Satan's humility could handle. He became so caught up in the thrill of worship that he began to desire it for himself. From that obsession grew the faulty reasoning that he somehow deserved to be worshiped. Was he not the most beautiful and perfect creature in God's creation? He was, but he was not God, who said to him, "Your heart was lifted up because of your beauty; you corrupted your wisdom for the sake of your splendor; I cast you to the ground, I laid you before kings, that they might gaze at you. . . . Therefore I brought fire from your midst; it devoured you, and I turned you to ashes upon the earth in the sight of all who saw you" (Ezek. 28:17–18).

What was Satan's problem? He wanted to be *like* God. Satan did not want to be *dependent* on God, but he wanted others dependent on him. Isaiah describes Satan's declaration of independence and subsequent fall this way:

How you are fallen from heaven, O Lucifer, son of the morning! How you are cut down to the ground, you who weakened the nations! For you have said in your heart: "I will ascend into heaven, I will exalt my throne above the stars of God; I will also sit on the mount of the congregation on the farthest sides of the north; I will ascend above the heights of the clouds, I will be like the Most High" (Isa. 14:12–14).

Satan was eager to go his own way. He didn't want to play second fiddle; he wanted to occupy first chair. But he couldn't. God wouldn't permit it, and the consequences were disastrous. God said, "Yet you shall be brought down to Sheol, to the lowest depths of the Pit" (Isa. 14:15). You would think that Satan would have seen the error of his ways with these warnings, but he didn't. He refused to have a repentant heart. In *Paradise Lost*, John Milton wonderfully captures Satan's attitude when he has him say, "Better to reign in hell than serve in heav'n."[3] What an accurate reflection of Satan's attitude as revealed in his activities—an unrepentant heart bent upon rebellion.

Angels' loss of significance

Satan couldn't bear to be insignificant in solitude. He had to try to rob the rest of God's creation of its significance as well. The only way he could do this was to entice others to follow his same foolish course of rebellion against God. Satan has proven himself a master at drawing others into his fight for independence, which God views as rebellion.

Apparently Satan's first effort to get others to join his rebellion was a grassroots effort. He sought to convince the rest of the angels that they would be better off if they declared their independence from God as well. Many fell for Satan's ploy. Revelation 12 uses the metaphor of a dragon to describe Satan. Verse 4 says, "His tail drew a third of the stars of heaven and threw them to the earth." Those stars were once God-fearing angels who fell under the spell of Satan's independence movement. Scripture continues,

And war broke out in heaven: Michael and his angels fought against the dragon; and the dragon and his angels fought, but they did not prevail, nor was a place found for them in heaven any longer. So the great dragon was cast out, that serpent of old, called the Devil and Satan, who deceives the whole world; he was cast to the earth, and his angels were cast out with him (vv. 7–9).

All of this means that Satan now has an army of fiends to help him carry out his insidious work of separating God's creation from its significance.

Man's loss of significance

With Satan's independence from God, and consequent insignificance, and with a host of rebellious angels at his side, it was only a matter of time until he would try to add men and women to his colleagues. It is interesting that Satan used the same feelings that destroyed him to trick Eve into losing her significance.

Satan first suggested to Eve that God was withholding something from her. Genesis 3:1 says, "Now the serpent was more cunning than any beast of the field which the LORD God had made. And he said to the woman, 'Has God indeed said, "You shall not eat of every tree of the garden"?'"

Satan knew better than that! He knew it was impossible for God not to be entirely trustworthy. But he implied that God could not be trusted. He suggested that the everlasting God was capable of withholding good from His most significant creation. It was preposterous, but Satan uses that line today as well. If God were capable of withholding good to our first parents, what makes us think He would not withhold good from us? If you are pondering this, you are a fish about to bite the most dangerous line you've seen.

While Eve's response in Genesis 3:2 attempted to set God's true boundaries ("We may eat the fruit of the trees of the garden"), she also bought into the idea that God was withholding something. She said God told her, "You shall not eat it, nor shall you touch it, lest you die." Her words inferred that God was so mean and strict that not only would He not allow them to eat the fruit, He wouldn't even let them touch it. But that is not what He had commanded (2:17).

Never one to miss an opportunity when he has his foot in the door, Satan went even further. He said, "You will not surely die. For God knows that in the day you eat of it your eyes will be opened, and you will be like God, knowing good and evil" (3:4-5). In other words, "Eve, you're certainly right. In fact, you can't trust God. God is a liar. God is just trying to scare you into submission. He wants you dependent on Him to build His ego. He's not interested in your good. He doesn't want you to discover how satisfying it is to be able to stand on your own like He does. He's selfish. He wants to keep that wonderful experience for Himself."

Eve swallowed that lie—hook, line and sinker. Genesis 3:6 says, "So when the woman saw that the tree was good for food, that it was pleasant to the eyes, and a tree desirable to make one wise, she took of its fruit and ate. She also gave to her husband with her, and he ate."

The lie that Satan proposed to Eve—that significance comes through independence—is still being communicated today. It goes something like this: Dependent people are weak and need a crutch. Those who get the most out of life don't need any help, and they certainly don't need God. They are wealthy (financially independent), self-confident (emotionally independent) and well established (socially independent). Sound familiar? If you are an American it does. That's the American dream! To be financially independent. To be politically independent. Now, even to be sexually independent. Independence from tyranny is good, but God is not a tyrant. Independence from God and God's will is not true independence; it's just dependence on an incapable source—yourself.

A loss of belonging

When Adam and Eve rebelled against God, certain consequences took place. Genesis 3:16-19 tells us,

To the woman He said: "I will greatly multiply your sorrow and your conception; in pain you shall bring forth children; your desire shall be for your husband, and he shall rule over you." Then to Adam He said, "Because you have heeded the voice of your wife, and have eaten from the tree of which I commanded you, saying, 'You shall not eat of it': 'Cursed is the ground for your sake; in toil you shall eat of it all the days of your life. Both thorns and thistles it shall bring forth for you, and you shall eat the herb of the field. In the sweat of your face you shall eat bread till you return to the ground, for out of it you were taken; for dust you are, and to dust you shall return.'"

In summary, because of the sin of Adam and Eve, the whole human race has to live with cursed ground (weeds and thorns grow much more readily than fruits and vegetables); hard labor (never again would the ground give of its bounty easily); pain in childbirth (child bearing had been God's plan all along but not with the accompanying pain); and conflict between the sexes (the word translated "desire" in Genesis 3:16 is from the primitive root *shuwq*, which means "to run over, flow over, overpower"). Mankind was the crown of God's creation, but the idyllic life was over. Eden was lost and so was man's significance.

With the loss of significance came the most tragic loss of all—loss of life. As a result of sin, Adam and Eve would not belong to each other forever. They would one day be separated from one another; they would die, and so would all their descendants. Genesis 5:5 reports that Adam lived to be 930 years old, but he did die. At the time of this writing, the oldest confirmed living person in the world today is Jeanne Calment of Arles, France, who is 121. But one day Jeanne will die also. We all will die and that, too, is part of the price we pay for our independence from God.

The Bible views death differently from they way many people view it today. Death in Scripture is not just the cessation of bodily functions; it's the breaking of our relationship with God.

The moment that Adam and Eve chose to disobey God, their relationship with Him was broken and they died immediately. This wasn't physical death—that took 930 years. It was relational death. When God came to the garden to walk with Adam and Eve after they had sinned, they hid themselves (Gen. 3:8). Instead of rushing to God in order to experience the relationship that had meant so much to them, they avoided Him. They had to, because their joy had been replaced by shame. The part of them that responded to God's love and fellowship was no longer operating. They were spiritually dead.

Furthermore, this broken relationship and its consequences have been passed down to every generation since then. Every person born since Adam and Eve is spiritually stillborn. We are alive physically, emotionally and intellectually, but we are dead spiritually. Our relationship with God was severed by sin — the sin in which we are born (Ps. 51:5) and the sin we perform every day (1 John 3:4). That's why the apostle Paul addresses the Ephesians as those who "were *dead* in trespasses and sins" (Eph. 2:1, italics mine). The Ephesians' relationship with God had been broken by sin, and a broken relationship with God is the root cause of insignificance. Unfortunately, we also are born with a broken relationship with God. We begin our lives with the most important part of our life dead, and for many people, the rest of life is spent waiting for the rest of their body to catch up.

Apart from God

This spiritual death changed us from creatures who

were dependent on their Creator to creatures who were forced to depend on themselves. We no longer belonged to God's family. We were compelled to deal with challenges that God never intended for us to face.

God never intended for man personally to experience evil. Now he would "know" not only good but also evil (Gen. 3:5). And the evils man has endured are almost beyond reckoning. Beginning with Cain and Abel, violent death has been man's intimate companion. Famines, earthquakes and pestilence have brought suffering and death to untold millions. The tragic loss of a child, the pain of cancer, the ravages of war are all experiences that man came to know because of his willful independence from God.

Now man also would have to protect himself. "And they heard the sound of the LORD God walking in the garden in the cool of the day, and Adam and his wife hid themselves from the presence of the LORD God among the trees of the garden" (Gen. 3:8). When fearful, they could no longer turn to the Lord. They had to find their own protection. The psalmist said, "The LORD is my rock and my fortress and my deliverer; my God, my strength, in whom I will trust; my shield and the horn of my salvation, my stronghold. I will call upon the LORD, who is worthy to be praised; so shall I be saved from my enemies" (Ps. 18:2-3). But this is true only for those who belong to God's family. All who choose to reject their relationship with God, all who want to rely on themselves and their independence, have no claim to this protection.

In addition, we now must answer to God for our actions.

When God confronted Adam with the questions, "Who told you that you were naked? Have you eaten from the tree of which I commanded you that you should not eat?" (Gen. 3:11), there was no one else to answer for him. How fearful a thing it is to stand before an all-knowing, all-powerful God and give account of ourselves and our independent actions. We can understand Job's desperation when he cried out, "For He is not a man, as I am, that I may answer Him, and that we should go to court together. Nor is there any mediator between us, who may lay his hand on us both" (Job 9:32–33).

When man abandoned the joy of belonging to God's family and went his own way, we lost our right to look to Him for any of our needs. The care and protection that once composed our significance in God became the first casualty of our rebellion.

Apart from our neighbors

With our relationship to God broken, all our other relationships suffered as well. As soon as disobedience appeared, so did blame and accusation. Adam blamed Eve ("The woman . . . she gave me of the tree, and I ate") and indirectly blamed God ("whom *You* gave to be with me," Gen. 3:12, italics mine). Eve blamed the serpent ("The serpent deceived me, and I ate," Gen 3:13). Independence from God is a quick teacher of how to point the finger of blame at everyone but ourselves.

Nothing in the generations since has changed. Have you noticed that nobody is ever at fault anymore? Nobody wants to take the blame for their wrong actions. Our independence from God has spawned an independence from responsibility. The treasurer of a mainline denomination embezzled $2.2 million and blamed the denomination for creating the stress that caused her to do it. An Anglican bishop claims that adultery is in the genes we inherited from our forefathers and thus behaving like animals isn't our fault. We blame everyone but ourselves.

In his book *Reality Therapy*, William Glasser tells of a boy named Aaron who was the most obnoxious child he had ever met. The boy would kick, scream, disrupt his classes and make everything as unpleasant as possible. Aaron, for his part, blamed his mother and everyone else for his behavior. It was only when he was held responsible for his actions that he changed in a remarkable way. He became courteous, well behaved and, for the first time in his life, was able to play constructively with other children.[4]

The outcome of shifting the blame is fractured (and sometimes broken) relationships. Trying to use someone else to hide your sins is wrong and creates tension in your relationship with that person. We become adversaries rather than friends. We experience rejection instead of belonging.

Facing the truth

The sin in the Garden of Eden didn't produce just a new outlook on life for Adam and Eve—it produced a new life. Sadly, it was a life independent from God. Once independent, they lost everything.

In certain places, the shape of the land creates an illusion that gravity is being defied. For example, near Los Angeles is a hill where many people stop their cars, put the gearshift in neutral and seemingly coast up hill. But if you were to put a plumb level on the ground where the cars "roll up hill," it would show that the cars are actually rolling downhill. Appearances can be deceiving.[5]

Unfortunately, Adam and Eve, and all of us who have followed them, have had to learn this the hard way. For Satan, independence looked like the road to significance, but it ended in a quagmire. The same was true for the angels who were deceived by Satan. The same is true for people today who are deceived by the father of lies. Instead of finding meaning, man has found only sorrow and regret.

The loss of a dependent relationship with God resulted in the loss of our significance. Adam and Eve found true significance only in what He made them, how He created them and in the way He crafted them for Himself. When they decided to live for themselves, they became independent and, unfortunately, insignificant. The consequences of this loss of significance have been seen ever since.

---

[1] David C. Needham, *Birthright* (Portland, Oreg.: Multnomah Press, 1979), p. 22.

[2] Donald Grey Barnhouse, *The Invisible War* (Grand Rapids, Mich.: Zondervan, 1965), p. 28.

[3] John Milton, *Paradise Lost, Book One* (New York: Odyssey Press, 1935), p. 262.

[4] William Glasser, *Reality Therapy* (New York: Harper & Row, 1965), pp. 135–140.

[5] Donald Grey Barnhouse, *Let Me Illustrate* (New Jersey: Fleming H. Revell, Co., 1967), p. 26.

Chapter 3

Belonging: The Search
for a Substitute

During the second week of December 1995, a series of three Pacific storms rumbled through southern California with pelting, torrential rains that caused more than $20 million in damages and knocked out power to tens of thousands of people. In the midst of these devastating storms, a 200-foot-wide sinkhole suddenly opened up in the seaside city of Del Mar, swallowing one home and threatening to destroy as many as 24 others. Apparently, water from the storms or a leaking water main had eroded the soil from underneath the home, allowing the sinkhole to form.

Yet a sinkhole big enough to swallow a house is small compared with the chasm Adam and Eve created between God and themselves. When they joined Satan's rebellious independence movement against God, they and all their descendants suddenly found themselves with the freedom to fall into the dark sinkhole of sin and destruction. No longer could they look to God for significance. When we lost a meaningful relationship with Him, we lost our most important reason to live. With that loss came an emptiness that has plagued us ever since. The resulting hole swallowed much more than a house; it swallowed the whole human race and left behind a void that seems impossible to fill and a helplessness that seems impossible to remove.

The search for significance

One of the chief objectives of Satan is to keep men and women from looking to God for their significance. To do that he seeks to convince us there is a significance (even a greater significance) apart from God. Satan doesn't care what we look to for significance, as long as it isn't God. Anything but God will do in Satan's scheme, and therefore he offers a smorgasbord of options for false significance. You may have tried some of these options:

Our abilities

This search for significance has led to the cult of the athlete. Athletics is not wrong, of course; in fact, athletics can be very enjoyable and satisfying. But the cult of the athlete is sinister, not satisfying.

Consider that the president of the United States earns an annual salary of $200,000 (this, of course, doesn't include all his "perks").[1] The average salary for a player in the NBA, on the other hand, is $2 million.[2] That's ten times more than the president makes. Some sports figures draw even larger salaries. NBA's top draft pick in 1994, Glenn Robinson, received a ten-year contract worth $68 million.[3] Cal Ripken Jr. of the Baltimore Orioles has a base pay of $6 million per year.[4] Even more money is made in the endorsement market, where a highly paid athlete pitches a product he or she may know little about. Celebrity endorsements is big business today.

Athletes command these exorbitant salaries because so many men, women and children are obsessed with sports. Sports figures are placed on a pedestal in the rarified air reminiscent of the ancient Greek gods. They are admired, even worshiped, and thought to be both invincible and above the law. Psychologist Carol Moog observed, "Americans have elevated celebrity and fame to such a ridiculous status, they can't accept it when a hero commits a crime." She made this statement in regard to a poll in which 1,240 adults were asked to name the athletes they most admire. On the list of those "most frequently mentioned" were O. J. Simpson (implicated in a double murder), Tonya Harding (who pleaded guilty to conspiracy in the attack on a skating rival) and Mike Tyson (a convicted rapist). They were not high on the list, but the fact that they made it at all reveals much about American values.[5]

If you have traveled to Cooperstown, New York, or even watched the ceremonies at which our baseball heroes are inducted into the Hall of Fame, you know that athletic ability is temporary. Even .300 hitters get old, tumble from their pedestal and are replaced by younger, seemingly more gifted athletes. When their ability is gone so is their significance, and all the athlete has left are his medals and his memories.

Our bodies

Sensuality surrounds us. John Leo, columnist for *U.S. News & World Report*, wrote about a series of ads produced by Calvin Klein. He observed, "Calvin Klein is at it again, this time with a series of bus and magazine ads showing young teens posed in what look like opening scenes from a porn movie. . . . Sex is rather blankly offered here as a commodity by and for the bombed-out and hopelessly numb. . . . It's not just in our face and totally inappropriate on buses and in magazines—it's decadent."[6] The more we strive to find our significance in our bodies, the more depraved we become.

Television is the primary promoter of sensuality. In *Disciplines of a Godly Man*, R. Kent Hughes says, "Men, it is the 'legal' sensualities, the culturally acceptable indulgences which will take us down. The long hours of indiscriminate TV watching, which is not only culturally cachet but is expected of the American male, is a massive culprit of desensitization."[7] Hughes also focuses on another source of sensuality. "The expected male talk—double entendre, coarse humor, laughter at things which ought to make us blush—is another deadly agent."[8]

Wherever we turn, human bodies are offered as the solution to filling our lack of significance. In her autobiography *Moving Pictures*, actress Ali McGraw describes her sad personal love stories. Of her affair with Steve McQueen, she recalls that five years with him brought her career to a standstill. The prenuptial agreement she signed ("I was so in love") meant she got nothing when it was over.

By then, he was having an affair and so was she. Her male "addiction," she says, led her to cheat on every man she was ever with. "This thing about male addiction—I HATE all this. It sounds so trendy, California, you know? But I believe a lot of us feel a kind of hole in our hearts. An unfortunate ache that's fixed by some people by eating too much. For others with freebase. In my case, I'm a romance junkie."[9] But, as Ali McGraw tragically discovered, her relationships were empty. She never found true significance in any of them.

Eventually the human body softens, sags and suffers. Those who find their significance in sensuality or sex, those who look for significance in the youthful contours of their body, have a rude awakening coming. You can't find significance in something as insignificant as the human body. There has to be something more.

Our position

During my lifetime I have seen a crack formed in the so-called glass ceiling. That means that the top rung of the ladder in the business and corporate world is finally opening to women. And while this change was a long time in coming, frequently it results in nothing more than doubling the number of candidates for failure in the search for significance.

Both men and women strive fiercely to climb the corporate ladder—often to find it leaning against the wrong wall. The average white-collar worker today works about 44 hours per week; male executives on average work 48.5

hours a week. These figures are higher than at anytime since World War II.[10]

Ann Landers, the well-known advice columnist, received a letter that reflects what many in the business world are finding out. It said:

"Please come home early." This was the most unreasonable request ever made by my wife of almost 40 years.

She didn't make this request often. It came mostly on Saturdays, Sundays and holidays, but it seemed that I always had so many things to do that in spite of her gentle urging, I rarely came home early.

I don't want to give the impression that I was never at home. I was at home a lot. We rarely did anything out of the ordinary. We enjoyed the kids and the grandchildren. We listened to music, read the paper and had meals together. Sometimes we would just talk about how the day had gone.

Now I know why she asked me so often to "Please come home early." She wasn't just lonely, she was lonely for me. When she passed away a short time ago, I learned firsthand what loneliness is all about.

I have a supportive family and many good friends. I'm free now to go places and do things, but I'm lonesome. Lonesome for her.

Now that she's gone, I've found the time to "come home early," but there is nobody to come home to.

There is nobody to do those simple little things with, such as watching the evening news, listening to music and reading the paper. And nobody cares how my day went.

If I should get a call from the good Lord to "Please come home early," I won't fight it.

— Lonesome in K. C.

It's unfortunate that it takes a tragedy for many people to realize how empty all those extra hours at the office really are.

Businesspeople in the United States are not the only ones blinded by this vain search for significance. A company in Tokyo called Japan Efficiency Headquarters is moving in to solve the problem of disintegrating family ties in Japan. For a modest $1,200 it rents out actors who go to visit elderly people whose families are too busy to visit them. For a few hours, the actors play the part of absent family members. The lonely senior citizens who receive this mock family reunion know that the participants are paid actors, but evidently they think this is better than no family reunion at all.[11]

Position is not the path to significance. Men and women have yet to learn that the key to the company car or their name on the company stationary can't bring the significance they are looking for. The emptiness they experience is far greater than any of this can fill.

Our accomplishments

Many people feel they can gain significance by racking up numerous accomplishments. What kind of accomplishments? Take your pick. Perhaps it's the long list of books they have written, awards they have won or records they have set. A man in Fontana, California, on April 24-25, 1993, set a world record by doing 46,001 pushups in a 24-hour period. A man in New Brighton, Minnesota, holds the pucker record; he kissed 8,001 people in 8 hours (one every 3.6 seconds) on September 15, 1990. Their feats got them into the *Guinness Book of World Records* and brought them their 15 minutes of fame. Yet did they fill the emptiness everyone feels? Were their feats really significant, eternally significant? Hardly. Besides, someone will come along someday who can do more pushups or kiss more people, and the senseless cycle will start all over again.

Maybe you're saying to yourself, *But these are just frivolous accomplishments.* You are right, they are frivolous. That's the point. All activities are frivolous. The only accomplishment that reconnects us to significance is the accomplishment at Calvary, where Jesus died for our sins and made it possible for our lost relationship with God to be restored. All other accomplishments fall in varying degrees into the category of the frivolous.

Our family

Of all the substitutes for significance discussed so far, this perhaps has the greatest merit and, therefore, the greatest danger. The family was created by God. Genesis

2:21-22 says, "And the LORD God caused a deep sleep to fall on Adam, and he slept; and He took one of his ribs, and closed up the flesh in its place. Then the rib which the LORD God had taken from man He made into a woman, and He brought her to the man." The family was God's idea to meet a part of Adam's needs. Yet the Fall of man and its accompanying loss of significance has twisted even this.

The U.S. Advisory Board on Child Abuse and Neglect estimates that 2,000 children, most of them under four years of age, die each year at the hands of their parents or caretakers. In fact, neglect and abuse kill more children than traffic accidents, drowning or falls.[12]

Worldwide, the situation is even worse. Action International Ministries reports that more than 100 million street children struggle to survive in cities—many of them through prostitution. In Bogota, Colombia, the number of prostitutes under the age of 13 has quintupled since 1987. Brazil now has more than 250,000 child prostitutes. Relief agencies in Thailand estimate that there are now 2 million prostitutes in that nation, with up to 800,000 of them being children under 16. The governments of these countries consider them "trash" and "disposable." Some policemen (and others) "moonlight" by contracting to kill street kids.[13] The world is not a friendly place for families.

The family is a God-given responsibility. The apostle Paul said, "If anyone does not provide for his own, and especially for those of his household, he has denied the faith and is worse than an unbeliever" (1 Tim. 5:8). But the family can only temporarily fill our need for significance.

Children grow up and leave home. Our spouse may die before we do. If our significance has been built upon those in our family, our latter years can be filled with loneliness and disillusionment. As important as the family is, when it is used to meet a need it was not intended to meet, the consequences are tragic.

In the last several decades conservative Christians have "rediscovered" family values. That's healthy. But with that discovery has come what some have called "the cult of the family." Even well-meaning Christians view their family as their primary responsibility, their reason to live. Often we hear that our family should be at the top of our priorities. But where does that place God? Jesus said, "He who loves father or mother more than Me is not worthy of Me. And he who loves son or daughter more than Me is not worthy of Me" (Matt. 10:37). The Master was not implying that we should not love our family, but that our love for family must be subordinate to our love for Him. When we focus so much on our relationship with our family that we fail to focus on our relationship with God, we are setting ourselves up for a painful fall into the sinkhole of insignificance. Children grow up and move away. Relatives disappoint us. But Jesus never fails. Real significance is found only in a right relationship with Him.

The ultimate futillity of the search

Many people spend most of their lives looking for significance in the world only to wake up one morning and realize they haven't found it. For these people, Satan has a special lie. He tells them, "Significance can't be found. It's futile to continue the search." The outcome of this lie is despair.

Clarence Darrow, who has been labeled "one of our most vocal atheists," was described candidly by one of his contemporaries, Harry Emerson Fosdick:

> To him the "outstanding fact" of human life is the utter "futility of it all"; he thinks that possibly "no life is of much value, and every death is little loss" to the world; he feels that the "most satisfactory part of life is the time spent in sleep, when one is utterly oblivious to existence" . . . The outstanding fact that cannot be dodged by thoughtful men is the futility of it all.[14]

Clarence Darrow is not alone in his despair. The philosopher Bertrand Russell was another man who had no use for the Bible or God. He said of life:

> The life of a man is a long march through the night, surrounded by invisible foes, tortured by weariness and pain, toward a goal which few can hope to reach and where none may tarry long. One by one as they march, our comrades vanish from our sight, seized by the silent orders of omnipotent death. Brief and powerless is man's life. On him and all his race the slow, sure doom falls, pitiless and dark. Blind to good and evil, reckless of destruction, omnipotent matter rolls on its relentless way. For man, condemned today to lose his dearest, tomorrow himself to pass through the gate of darkness, it

remains only to cherish, ere yet the blow falls, the lofty thoughts that ennoble his little day.

The well-known author H. G. Wells also rejected the truth of the Gospel. As he neared the end of his life he was filled with despair. Critics describe his final literary work as a "scream of despair." Wells himself said, "Despair is a frightful queerness . . . that there is no way out, or around, or through the impasse. It is the end."

F. Scott Fitzgerald, another man who never found significance in Christ Jesus, described despair from personal experience. He said, "In a really dark night of the soul it is always three in the morning, day after day." The only alternatives to the loss of significance are the darkness of despair or the light of the Gospel.

When faced with the dark emptiness of despair, many people choose what they think is the only way out—suicide. John Wesley White commented, "I think the saddest note I've ever read was written by actor Hugh Pryor just before he shot himself in Las Vegas. The note read, 'Tell my friends I'll meet them in hell.'"[15] It's sad how insignificance warps the mind!

Because so many people are feeling insignificant today, suicide is a growing problem, especially among teenagers. A poll reported by *USA Today* finds:

A third of U.S. teenagers say they have considered suicide, 15% have thought seriously about it, and 6% have actually tried, a Gallup Poll says. Suicides by 15- to 19-year-olds, which have tripled in the past 30 years to 10 per 100,000, are the second-leading cause of death for that group, says the National Institute of Mental Health. Accidents are first. The study of 1,152 13- to 19-year-olds is the first national documentation on teens' views of suicide. Among the respondents, 51% were male, 49% female.[16]

The farther we move from God, the deeper the darkness and despair grow. The more we try to find our significance in our bodies, our families or our accomplishments, the less true significance we discover. The more we suffer from a failure to find true significance, the darker our world becomes. But there is a positive side to this. Oswald Chambers observed, "When a man gets to despair, he knows that all his thinking will never get him out, he will only get out by the sheer creative effort of God; consequently, he is in the right attitude to receive from God that which he cannot gain for himself."

As the world grows more despairing, Christians have an opportunity to share God's solution to the futile search for significance. As the emptiness of man's heart increases, so does his need to find the only cure for that emptiness. As men and women try "new and improved" ways to satisfy their search for significance and fail in the process, the more reasonable God's alternative becomes. There is a way to restore our significance. It is God's way, the only way. We will explore this way in the next chapter.

[1] *American Wages and Salary Survey*, 3rd ed., 1995.

[2] "David Falk: an offensive threat for NBA players," *U.S. News & World Report*, December 11, 1995, p. 78.

[3] Ibid.

[4] "Strange Solidarity," *Fortune*, May 15, 1995, p. 144.

[5] *USA Today*, quoted in *Pulpit Helps*, August 1995.

[6] John Leo, "Decadence, the corporate way," *U.S. News & World Report*, August 28–September 4, 1995, p. 31.

[7] R. Kent Hughes, *Disciplines of a Godly Man* (Wheaton, Ill.: Crossway Books, 1991), p. 25.

[8] Ibid.

[9] Ann Trebbe, *USA Today*, April 4, 1991, p. 20.

[10] "Forty hour work week not what it use to be," *Lincoln Journal Star*, October 29, 1994, p. 6.

[11] "And You Must Be . . . Mom?" *Newsweek*, June 29, 1992, p. 8.

[12] "Parents Who Kill Their Children," *U.S. News & World Report*, May 8, 1995, p. 14.

[13] Doug Nichols, *Are Street Children "Trash"?* (Bothel, Wash.: Action International Ministries).

[14] Harry Emerson Fosdick, *As I See Religion* (Westport, Conn.: Greenwood Press, 1975), pp. 178-179.

[15] John Wesley White, *Survivors* (Eugene, Oreg.: Harvest House, 1983), p. 59.

[16] Karen S. Peterson, *USA Today*, May 2, 1995, p. A-1.

Chapter 4

Belonging: The Triumph of Restoration

One afternoon the members of a health club assembled for a meeting on nutrition and exercise. The dietitian leading the discussion asked each member to describe his or her daily routine. The first participant admitted to a number of excesses, including overeating. Others joined in agreement. But one seriously overweight member reported, "I eat healthily and moderately. I drink only water and I exercise frequently." "I see," said the dietitian. "Are you sure you have nothing else to tell us?" "Well, yes," said the man. "I also lie extensively."

Unlike this person, God does not have the capacity for deception. He has never attempted to keep any secrets from us. He has never instituted any cover-up to prevent us from finding our way back to significance. As the songwriter Stuart Hamblen claims, "It is no secret what God can do." From the beginning God devised a plan for us to regain our place in His family, the place that we lost through Adam and Eve's rebellion. God's desire is that we experience the joy of belonging, and ever since the day we lost that joy His intention has been that we should belong again.

Restoration started with God

Man's fall began with Satan, but our restoration started with God. The apostle Paul claimed the plan to regain the joy of belonging originated long before man was created. He told the Christians at Ephesus, "Blessed be the God and Father of our Lord Jesus Christ, who has blessed us with every spiritual blessing in the heavenly places in Christ, *just as He chose us in Him before the foundation of the world*, that we should be holy and without blame before Him in love" (Eph. 1:3–4, italics mine).

The apostle Peter said of our redemption, "Knowing that you were not redeemed with corruptible things, like silver or gold, from your aimless conduct received by tradition from your fathers, but with the precious blood of Christ, as of a lamb without blemish and without spot. *He indeed was foreordained before the foundation of the world*, but was manifest in these last times for you" (1 Pet. 1:18-20, italics mine).

And the apostle John wrote, "All who dwell on the earth [the unsaved] will worship him [the Beast], whose names have not been written in the Book of Life of *the Lamb slain from the foundation of the world*" (Rev. 13:8, italics mine). Before we were created, before we sinned, God knew that we would need a plan for restoration, and in His great love for us He devised one.

When Adam and Eve sinned, God was not surprised. He knew mankind would follow Satan's lead and break our relationship with Him. He was well aware of how we would join Satan's rebellion and sever our dependence on Him. So

God devised a plan in eternity past that required man to have an absolute dependency on Him in order to find true significance. This was not done out of pride; it was done out of love. God knew that only by experiencing a dependence on Him would we gain a sense of belonging. Through this belonging we in turn would gain a sense of significance. God didn't have to resort to Plan B or Plan C. Only one plan was necessary.

God's plan to restore to us the joy of belonging is first revealed in Genesis 3:15. He told the serpent (or Satan), "I will put enmity between you and the woman, and between your seed and her Seed; He shall bruise your head, and you shall bruise His heel." This was not Eve's "seeds" (plural, meaning all her descendants) but her "Seed" (singular, meaning the Messiah, Jesus Christ). The plan God conceived before He formed the earth was now set in motion. It clearly reflects His character, for only a gracious, loving God could have devised a strategy that would restore the joy of belonging to Him.

We must exclude all those who might be pretenders to the divine drawing board. No one but God could have or would have devised a plan to enable us to regain our lost significance. This exclusion includes:

Satan

If God were Satan, He would have no desire for a redemptive plan. When Satan challenged God and lost, he knew there was no hope for him. He is a powerful enemy, but even his victories are hollow. Whatever bravado he continues to put forward today is just a facade. Satan is a toothless enemy. He is like a little boy held by the scruff of his neck, kicking and flailing and even landing a few of his punches, but not able to put his opponent down for the count.

Satan's desire, however, is to see as many of us as possible join him in his ultimate punishment. He is such an evil and malicious being that the little enjoyment he can salvage out of his doomed rebellion is comprised of robbing God of as many souls as possible. Satan still "walks about like a roaring lion, seeking whom he may devour" (1 Pet. 5:8). No, Satan does not desire our restoration; he actively seeks our destruction. He has no plan to reconnect our relationship with God. In fact, his plan is to do all in his power to prevent our return to God. Restoring the joy of belonging is God's plan, not Satan's.

Angels

If God were an angel, He would have no understanding of a redemptive plan. When Satan rebelled, Scripture says that "His tail drew a third of the stars of heaven and threw them to the earth" (Rev. 12:4). These are called "fallen angels" or "demons." They sided with Satan in the rebellion and now serve him in his efforts to destroy mankind. Still, there are myriads of angels in heaven who did not rebel. First Peter 1:12 says that it was made known to the Old Testament prophets that some of the revelations they received (such as the Messianic Psalms) were for future times and not for their own. Perhaps these men looked in puzzlement at such expressions as, "He guards all his bones; not one of them is broken" (Ps. 34:20), or, "They divide My garments among them, and for My clothing they cast lots" (22:18). Not only did the prophets wonder about such things, but Peter says that even the angels were curious about the way God would accomplish our salvation.

Peter implies that our redemption is so great a mystery that even the angels don't understand it. And why should they? God's plan of salvation is for men and women, not for angels. The angels who sinned have not had their relationship with God restored by Christ's blood. Jesus died for you and me, not for angels. God did not become an angel to redeem angels; He became a human being to redeem human beings. In a way that we don't fully understand, God the Son was infused into the womb of Mary to be born of a woman, yet without sin. He shrank His deity to fit into a human body without compromising either that deity or his humanity. Then the eternal Son experienced death at the hands of His creation that He might redeem them from sin and restore them to God.

How could we blame the angels for not understanding? You and I are the recipients of this marvelous plan and we don't understand everything about it either, but God does. God has crafted a plan that draws investigation from the curious hosts of heaven, but one they could never have devised. Restoring the joy of belonging is God's plan, not the angels.

Mankind

If God the Father were a man, He would have neither the ability to conceive of a plan to restore His lost significance nor the power to execute it. Certainly He would have a desire to do so, just no ability or power. The apostle Paul says that "we ourselves groan within ourselves, eagerly waiting for the adoption, the redemption of our body" (Rom. 8:23). We want so much to be delivered from sin that we can almost taste it, but we can do nothing about our desire. Romans 5:6 says, "For when we were still without strength, in due time Christ died for the ungodly." No man has the strength to gain his own salvation. Only God can restore the joy of belonging.

Certainly men have tried to recover this joy. They have followed their own agendas, as we saw in the last chapter; they have created their own achievements. But they have listened to the wrong voice, followed the wrong signals and failed miserably.

Author G. B. Robeson tells the story of a man lost in the jungle, desperately trying to find his way to safety. His strength was ebbing as the insects and stifling heat did their deadly work. Suddenly he heard what sounded like a bell tolling in the distance. *Surely*, he thought, *I am near civilization*. If he followed the sound of the bell he would be saved. Valiantly he struggled on, but he never seemed to draw closer to the sound. Finally he fell to the ground exhausted, never to rise again.

What had happened? Where did the sound of the bell come from? The mysterious bellbird had claimed another victim! According to Mr. Robeson, many travelers in the heart of the rain forest of Central and South America have been led to their death by the uncanny call of this seldom-seen bird. The bellbird's sound is so enticing that it produces an almost overpowering temptation to seek the source. But the sound of the bellbird will never lead to safety—only to exhaustion and inevitable destruction.

Anyone seeking to discover the path to his salvation is following a similar delusion and will experience the same fate. Proverbs says, "There is a way that seems right to a man, but its end is the way of death" (Prov. 14:12). We don't have the power to find our way back to God. Our minds are muddled about spiritual things and our eyes are blinded by Satan. Our plans to be restored to God only lead further from Him. Restoring the joy of belonging is God's plan, not ours.

Earthly gods

Adam and Eve must have intuitively known that their significance was tied to their relationship with God. Whether we like to admit it or not, we know the same thing. When man broke his relationship with God, he attempted to recapture his lost sense of belonging by creating his own gods. Taking wood, silver, gold and precious stones, he fashioned images on which he tried to depend. The prophet Isaiah described the situation with amazing accuracy when he said of man:

He hews down cedars for himself, and takes the cypress and the oak; he secures it for himself among the trees of the forest. He plants a pine, and the rain nourishes it.

Then it shall be for a man to burn, for he will take some of it and warm himself; yes, he kindles it and bakes bread; indeed he makes a god and worships it; he makes it a carved image, and falls down to it.

He burns half of it in the fire; with this half he eats meat; he roasts a roast, and is satisfied. He even warms himself and says, "Ah! I am warm, I have seen the fire."

And the rest of it he makes into a god, his carved image. He falls down before it and worships it, prays to it and says, "Deliver me, for you are my god!" (Isa. 44:14-17).

In other words, Isaiah says it is sheer foolishness to go out and cut down a tree, use part of it for the common tasks of heating the home and cooking food, but then take the other part and make a god out of it. No matter how intricately the god might be carved or how devoutly it might be worshiped, it still is just a piece of wood.

Such gods are incapable of thought. They cannot have concern for us, weep for us or love us. They are only inanimate objects. They are only manmade idols. They can no more devise a plan of redemption than the man in the moon. Hideyoshi, a Japanese warlord who ruled over Japan in the late 1500s, commissioned a colossal statue of Buddha for a shrine in Kyoto. It took 50,000 men five years to build, but the work had scarcely been completed when the earthquake of 1596 brought the roof of the shrine crashing down and wrecked the statue. In a rage Hideyoshi shot an arrow at the fallen idol. "I put you here at great expense," he shouted, "and you can't even look after your own temple!"

Today our earthly gods are automobiles, jobs, jewelry, fame, prominence, success, etc. They bring fleeting pleasure, but they do not bring lasting satisfaction and they certainly do not bring significance. Restoring the joy of belonging is the God of heaven's plan, not the plan of the unsatisfying gods of this earth.

Let God be God

After you have eliminated the rest of creation as the source of restoring joy, it brings you back to where you started: relying on God, your Creator, Sustainer and Redeemer. Some people try to have it all. They want the independence of saying, "I did it my way." Yet they also want to go to heaven when they die. These are opposing desires. Such people develop what might be called a "loophole mentality" in their relationship with God. I have heard that when comedian W. C. Fields was on his deathbed, a visitor found him reading the Bible. Asked what he was doing, he replied, "Looking for loopholes, my friend. Looking for loopholes." But Fields was a fool. There are no loopholes, just as there are no alternative plans to restoring the joy of belonging. Only God could conceive of redemption's plan, and only He has the wisdom and power to carry it out.

How are we to discover God's plan to restore our joy of belonging to Him? How are we to learn of the only way we can find true significance among the insignificant things of this world? We have to come back to the Bible. It alone explains how God's plan works. If you want to be significant, if you want to belong, find out what God says in His Word. His plan is worth considering.

How God's plan works

A plan is only good if it works. No matter how beautiful the face of a clock might look, if it can't tell time it's no good. God's plan for our redemption does work. In fact, here are just some of the steps He took to make sure His redemptive plan would work.

He executed the plan Himself

The best of plans can go awry if the person selected to carry out the details makes a mistake—even a well-intentioned mistake. For example, a hospital in Florida was required to stop all elective surgeries due to a series of errors. These included amputating the wrong foot of a diabetic, doing arthroscopic surgery on the wrong knee of another patient and removing the wrong patient from a ventilator, thereby causing his death.[1] No one intended for these blunders to happen—they were simply the results of human misjudgments and mistakes. But unintentional or not, they still cost great pain and heartache, and even the life of one patient. A good plan can be ruined by an incompetent person carrying it out.

God takes no chances with mistakes. Not only did He conceive of the perfect plan to restore our joy of belonging, but since He is the only perfect Being, He took it upon Himself to administer His plan personally. God did not entrust His redemption plan to seraphim, cherubim, pastors, priests or rabbis.

The apostle John tells us, "In the beginning was the Word, and the Word was with God, and the Word was God. . . . And the Word became flesh and dwelt among us, and we beheld His glory, the glory as of the only begotten of the Father, full of grace and truth" (John 1:1, 14). Why did God the Word come to be with us? Jesus said, "The Son of Man has come to seek and to save that which was lost" (Luke 19:10). Executing God's plan of restoration, redemption and salvation is so important that He choose to entrust it to no one but Himself. He wanted to insure we could find our way back to significance.

He required death in exchange for life

Many people emphasize the truth that God is love (1 John 4:8, 16). Without a doubt this is very important. But God is no indiscriminate lover. He loves the whole world but He is also just. His love must be balanced with His sense of justice. In fact, love cannot exist apart from justice. If a judge were to release a condemned, unrepentant murderer, we might say that he was loving to the murderer. But what about the victim's family? Would they perceive the judge as loving? I doubt it. If God is to demonstrate His love toward all, He must be just toward all.

Such justice requires that God follow His law. He cannot act capriciously; God must be true to the dictates of His own commandments. The Law declared, "'For the life of the flesh is in the blood, and I have given it to you upon the altar to make atonement for your souls; for it is the blood that makes atonement for the soul'" (Lev. 17:11). And Hebrews 9:22 says, "According to the law almost all things are purged with blood, and without shedding of blood there is no remission."

Blood represented life. When blood was shed, the ultimate price had been paid. No one understood that better than God. Jesus shed His blood—from His nail-pierced hands and feet, from His thorn-pierced brow and from the wound of His spear-punctured side. God the Son was the only perfect sacrifice that could be offered for our sin, and when Jesus bled and died at Calvary, the requirement of God's Law was met for all time. God had met the standard of His Law; He had sacrificed His Son in love. Belonging to God was now possible again.

Man's soul could not be restored to God's family any other way. Jesus had to die for us. When Jesus went to the Garden of Gethsemane for the last time, John writes that He "went out with His disciples over the Brook Kidron" (John 18:1). A drain ran from the temple altar down to the Kidron ravine to take away the blood of the sacrifices. It was Passover time, when more than 200,000 lambs were slain by the priests of Israel. When Jesus crossed the Kidron, it would have been red with the blood of many of these lambs. What a graphic reminder that His own blood would have to be shed if we were to be restored to God. Only the shed blood of God's Lamb could restore our significance.

He accepted nothing less than perfection

Hebrews 9:11-14 says,

> But Christ came as High Priest of the good things to come, with the greater and more perfect tabernacle not made with hands, that is, not of this creation. Not with the blood of goats and calves, but with His own blood He entered the Most Holy Place once for all, having obtained eternal redemption. For if the blood of bulls and goats and the ashes of a heifer, sprinkling the unclean, sanctifies for the purifying of the flesh, how much more shall the blood of Christ, who through the eternal Spirit offered Himself without spot to God, cleanse your conscience from dead works to serve the living God?

The lamb offered for sacrifice to God had to be without blemish. When people brought less-than-perfect animals for sacrifice, God was angered. He asked, "And when you offer the blind as a sacrifice, is it not evil? And when you offer the lame and sick, is it not evil? Offer it then to your governor! Would he be pleased with you? Would he accept you favorably?" . . . But now entreat God's favor, that He may be gracious to us. While this is being done by your hands, will He accept you favorably?" (Mal. 1:8–9). There could be no compromise. For God to accept a sacrifice, it had to be spotless and without flaw.

Do you know anyone without a flaw? I don't. Is there any flaw in your life? Have you ever been stained by sin? Of course you have. We all have. Not even the great men of the Bible were prefect. Abraham lied twice (Gen. 12:11-20;

20:2-13). Moses killed a man (Ex. 2:12). David committed adultery (2 Sam. 11:4). The list goes on and on. So if the blood of bulls and goats and the ashes of heifers are insufficient to pay for your sin, and no human being is perfect enough to atone for your sin (Heb. 10:4), that leaves you in quite a predicament. Where on earth would God find a perfect sacrifice whose blood could atone for sin? Nowhere on earth. That's why God supplied His own sacrifice. He sent to earth His only begotten Son, the only one who would be both sufficient and spotless. He offered His Son, Jesus.

Without God there would be no hope. Hope is not just a possibility; it is a certainty. In the Bible, *hope* is almost always a noun, not a verb. It's something we have, not something we do. Unlike those who hope their religion will get them into heaven, the Christian's hope is a guaranteed surety. We have this certainty because our hope is based on Jesus Christ. Colossians 1:27 says, "To them God willed to make known what are the riches of the glory of this mystery among the Gentiles: which is *Christ in you, the hope of glory*" (italics mine). We know for certain that someday we will be restored to the glory from which we fell when Adam and Eve chose to sin.

Furthermore, 1 Peter 1:3 says, "Blessed be the God and Father of our *Lord Jesus Christ, who according to His abundant mercy has begotten us again to a living hope* through the resurrection of Jesus Christ from the dead" (italics mine). Satan held mankind in bondage to the fear of death since the days of Adam and Eve. Now, with Jesus' death, burial and resurrection, we have a hope that lives. We do not look to a dead man for this hope, but to One who is alive, raised from the dead and ever living to make intercession for us to God.

Perhaps the most beloved verse in the Bible says it best: "For God so loved the world that He gave his only begotten Son, that whoever believes in Him should not perish but have everlasting life" (John 3:16). At Calvary, where Jesus died on the cross for our sins, the search for significance ended in victory. At Calvary, the great gap between God and His disobedient creation was closed. At Calvary, as all the demons of hell looked on, Jesus did what Satan tried so long and hard to keep Him from doing—He paid the penalty for our sins and made it possible for us once again to experience the joy of belonging to God.

Beginning again

Every person who is honest with himself has to admit that we have been searching for significance in all the wrong places. There is only one place to look for real purpose in life, just as there is only place to look for salvation. Jesus said, "I am the way, the truth, and the life. No one comes to the Father except through Me" (John 14:6). The significance we lost when we disobeyed the Father can be regained only through the One who perfectly obeyed the Father (Rom. 5:18–19). True significance is found in a relationship with God, a relationship that was broken by sin and can be restored only by Jesus.

If you have tried everything under the sun to find your significance and found it was all futile, admit that you have failed. That's the first step in succeeding. Admit that you cannot save yourself from sin and you cannot gain true significance on your own. Then tell God that you agree with Him. Tell Him that you believe only through Jesus Christ and His death at Calvary's cross on your behalf can the joy of belonging to God be restored. And when you tell Him, ask Him to save you from your sins so you can begin again.

The Bible says, "Believe on the Lord Jesus Christ, and you will be saved" (Acts 16:31). God doesn't require that you keep the Ten Commandments or join a church or turn over a new leaf to start over. But He does require that you trust what Jesus did on your behalf at Calvary to regain your significance. If you believe that God will save you if you ask Him, and if you believe that Jesus is the only way to be saved and you ask Him, I know He will save you. He saved me in that same way. I now have the joy of belonging to God. I have regained the significance lost because of my sin and rebellion. You can regain your significance too. Trust Jesus Christ as your Savior and discover the joy of belonging to the family of God.

---

[1] "Mistake-prone Florida hospital told to suspend elective surgery," *Lincoln Journal Star*, April 8, 1995, p. 21.

Chapter 5

Belonging: The Outcome of a New Creation

Many years ago there was a commercial on television for a soap that claimed it could "make you so clean, your mother wouldn't know you." While that is a dubious claim for a bar of soap, it is true when you receive Christ as your Savior. When you place your trust in Jesus, you don't become a new and improved model of yourself—you become a totally new creature, a whole new species of man. I know of many instances where a son or daughter who had been wild and reckless comes to trust Christ as Savior, and their own mother doesn't even recognize them as the child they were before.

In John 3 is the story of a man named Nicodemus, a Pharisee, a ruler of the Jews, who discovered this for himself. He came to see Jesus at night, and as they talked Jesus said to him, "Unless one is born again, he cannot see the kingdom of God" (v. 3). Nicodemus responded, "How can a man be born when he is old? Can he enter a second time into his mother's womb and be born?" (v. 4).

That was a legitimate question for someone who didn't understand what Jesus was talking about. Recognizing that Nicodemus hadn't grasped the truth, Jesus explained,

"Most assuredly, I say to you, unless one is born of water [physical birth] and the Spirit [spiritual birth], he cannot enter the kingdom of God" (v. 5). Those who are born physically are one species; those who are born spiritually are another. In order to understand the tremendous changes that occur when we receive Christ — our new identity and our new significance in Him — we have to understand the way we were before we were born again.

The way we were

Chances are, when you trusted Christ as Savior, no surprising physical changes took place. You didn't suddenly lose weight or grow taller. That's not what being "born again" or, more literally, "born from above" is all about. Salvation is a spiritual transformation, not a physical change. Spiritually, we can hardly appreciate where we are until we understand where we have come from.

Paul reminded the Gentile (non-Jewish) believers living at Ephesus where they were spiritually before they came to Christ as Savior: "Therefore remember that you, once Gentiles in the flesh . . . were without Christ, being aliens from the commonwealth of Israel and strangers from the covenants of promise, having no hope and without God in the world" (Eph. 2:11–12). Talk about insignificance! This drives home the great emptiness, the lack of belonging, that mankind experienced after Adam and Eve's sin—especially for the Gentile world. The word that best describes us is *without*. We were:

Without Christ

Christ (*christos*) is the Greek word for *Messiah* (*messiach*) in Hebrew. The Messiah is the One anointed by God and empowered by His Spirit to deliver His people from their enemies and establish His kingdom. In Jewish thought, the Messiah would be the king of the Jews, a political leader who would rise up to defeat the enemies of Israel and usher in a golden age of peace and prosperity. In Christian thought, the Messiah is the One who defeats the enemies of God and delivers His people from the consequences of their sin. Both Jewish and Christian thinking merge in the Person of Jesus Christ as present Savior and future King.

But the Gentiles were without Christ. That means they were without a champion to defeat their enemies. They were without the promise of peace or prosperity. They were abandoned to suffer the consequences of their sin. They were left without a Savior, and consequently they were left without significance. They were empty, without a future. They had no one to follow but humanity, and they knew that this leadership had already failed in the Garden of Eden.

Without citizenship

Without Christ, the Gentiles also were without citizenship. They did not belong to the nation of Israel. They were stateless. They were aliens.

An alien may reside in a city or country, but it is not *his* city or *his* country. He is not a citizen. As a non-citizen, he does not have the same privileges as the citizens of a country. Aliens usually cannot vote or participate in the decision-making process of a nation. They must passively accept the decisions of those who belong there. Furthermore, they are seen as transitory. Even though they may stay for a long time, since they do not "belong" there, they are not viewed as permanent. Aliens also face many uncertainties. They may be deported, their possessions may be confiscated, or they may even be killed if those in authority should decide to do so (Esther 3)—all without legal recourse.

Paul says that the Gentile world was alien from the "commonwealth of Israel." In theory, Israel was a theocracy, a government whose ultimate authority was God. Those who lived under the one He oppointed as ruler and kept His laws were blessed by Him. In practice, however, many of the kings of Israel failed to govern according to God's Law. They knew what they should do but didn't do it. The Gentiles, on the other hand, were almost completely ignorant of the Law. They were excluded from the Temple (except for the outermost court known as the Court of the Gentiles), they were snubbed by the Jews who saw them as socially inferior, and they were considered spiritually "unclean." Such exclusion gave Gentiles little opportunity to find out about God. They were aliens, outcasts, foreigners to all of God's blessings.

Before we received Christ as our Savior, we were in the same condition. There is a people of God (the Church[1]), but we didn't belong with them. We may have attended services in a church building, perhaps we even joined as a member, but we were aliens in God's sight nonetheless. We belonged to *a* church, but we didn't belong to Him and therefore didn't belong to *His* Church. We had no claim on God's protection and no true right to use the name "Christian."

Without covenant promises

The only thing worse than being an alien in Jewish society was being a stranger. Strangers were friendless. They were even more transitory than aliens. Strangers were only travelers on their way to someplace else (Paul uses the word *xenos*, which means a "guest"). If they ran out of money, strangers might remain in one place long enough to earn some travel money, but their stay was never for long. They were wanderers—restless and rootless.

Before we came to know Christ, we, too, were restless. We had no roots, no citizenship, no relationship with God. We were always traveling, always searching, always looking but never finding the answers. There was a God-shaped void in our hearts. As Saint Augustine said, "O, God, thou has formed us for Thyself, and our souls can know no rest until they rest in Thee."

Like tumbleweeds, we never attached ourselves to anything and especially not to God's promises. The word Paul uses for "promises" is *epaggelia*, which means "divine assurance of good." For those who are part of His household, God promises that "all things work together for good" (Rom. 8:28). Such promises do not apply to those who are only passing through.

Before we trusted Christ and found the joy of belonging to the family of God, we were always on the outside looking in. We were like the little boy who came from an impoverished family. He received no gifts at Christmas, but he often looked into the store windows at the fascinating toys other little boys could have. One day he was hit by a car and was taken to a hospital. As he recovered from the accident, one of the nurses sensed the boy's loneliness and longing for something to play with. So she brought him some toys—a troop of soldiers. As he touched them, he choked back a tear and said, "There isn't any glass between!"

When we receive Christ, we no longer are strangers to God's promises. Suddenly all those assurances that we looked at through the barrier of unbelief come within our grasp. The glass is gone. Nothing stands between us and enjoying all the blessings God has to offer. No longer are we outsiders, strangers looking in, but we are insiders who belong to God and whose promises belong to us.

Without hope

Before our salvation we were separate from Christ, separate from the blessings of God on His people, separate from the promises of God. As tragic as this is, without Christ we also were without hope, and that may be the biggest tragedy of all. But now that we have come to Christ, we have hope. But what kind of hope? What is biblical hope?

In the Bible hope isn't just a "hopefulness" but rather a

certainty. When we were not part of God's family or His promises, we had no certainty. Now all that has changed. With the joy of belonging comes the joy of hope.

Joseph Bayly, in his book *The View From a Hearse*, relates a conversation he had with a woman whose young son was dying:

> "It's good to know, isn't it," I spoke slowly, choosing my words with unusual care, "that even though the medical outlook is hopeless, we can have hope for our children in such a situation. We can be sure that after our child dies, he'll be completely removed from sickness and suffering and everything like that, and be completely well and happy."

> "If I could only believe that," the woman replied. "But I don't. When he dies, I'll just have to cover him up with dirt and forget I ever had him."[2]

Sadly, this woman's words express the hopeless plight of many people around us. They have no hope for their loved ones or for themselves. When you ask those without a personal relationship with Jesus Christ if they are going to heaven, they commonly answer, "I hope so." They are not sure, and how can they be? They are only engaging in wishful thinking. That's not enough for me. That's not real hope.

A Christian, on the other hand, can say with certainty, "Yes, I am going to heaven when I die." We have that hope because we are part of God's family. John 1:12–13 says, "But as many as received Him, to them He gave the right to become children of God, even to those who believe in

His name: who were born, not of blood, nor of the will of the flesh, nor of the will of man, but of God." God will not exclude any member of His family from heaven. His Son died so that all who trust Him as Savior could be as certain of heaven as if they were already there.

Furthermore, we can say "yes" with certainty because we can claim God's promises. First John 5:13 notes one of those promises: "These things I have written to you who believe in the name of the Son of God, that you may *know* that you have eternal life, and that you may continue to believe in the name of the Son of God" (italics mine). A Christian who has experienced the new birth doesn't have to wonder if he is going to heaven. We have God's Word on it!

Without spiritual life

Paul says we were "without God" when we were unbelievers. God was not a part of our lives. We were godless. In fact, spiritual things didn't make sense to us then. Paul says, "But the natural man does not receive the things of the Spirit of God, for they are foolishness to him; nor can he know them, because they are spiritually discerned" (1 Cor. 2:14).

Instead of living in the power of the Spirit of God, "we . . . conducted ourselves in the lusts of our flesh, fulfilling the desires of the flesh and of the mind, and were by nature children of wrath, just as the others" (Eph. 2:3). Before we were restored to God in redemption, we had no spiritual sensitivity. We sought only the things of the flesh.

Most of the world today is just like that—flesh-oriented. They follow the beck and call of their senses. Nowhere is this more evident than in the entertainment industry. In a letter written to advice columnist Ann Landers, a mother describes an episode on a late afternoon soap opera:

> A pretty teen-age girl is in bed with her boyfriend. The girl's mother walks in, catches them in the act and becomes extremely upset. The girl then gives a long speech on "the beauty of young love." She berates her mother for making something so special seem cheap and trashy. The mother appears to be ashamed of herself and apologizes for chastising her daughter.
>
> I ask you, Ann Landers, what kind of message is THAT?
>
> But this is not the end of the story. I suddenly realized that my five-year-old daughter was also in the room, watching the soap. I turned to her (embarrassed) and said, "In real life, honey, a boy and girl don't get in bed together that fast." She answered, "Oh, I know. They have a glass of wine first."[3]

Television used to be called a "vast wasteland"; now it is more like a "toxic wasteland"—poisonous as well as barren.

Much of the entertainment field is without spiritual life and therefore unbalanced in everything it does. In March 1995 the Media Research Center reported that the five major evening news programs in 1993 aired 18,000 stories, with only 211 having religious content (excluding stories about the siege of the Branch Davidian compound near Waco and the World Trade Center bombing). Of those, only 134 were taped pieces featuring a reporter; the remainder were short stories read by the news anchor.[4]

It is obvious that without the regeneration of the Holy Spirit, the natural man has no interest in spiritual matters. His heart is filled with sensuality and, as Jesus said, "out of the abundance of the heart the mouth speaks" (Matt. 12:34). This is the way we all were before we regained our significance in Christ.

A new species

But when we recognize our sin and our thirst for independence from God, when we repent and ask Jesus Christ to save us, we become a new person. In fact, God's redemptive plan doesn't simply give mankind a new start; it creates a whole new species. Second Corinthians 5:17 says, "Therefore, if anyone is in Christ, he is a new creation; old things have passed away; behold, all things have become new." We aren't just a new person; we are a new kind of person.

This verse tells us three facts about our new standing in Christ:

We are inhabitable

One of the concerns of conservationists is the fast pace at which habitats for certain species of wildlife are being changed into habitats for humans. Bogs are being filled, swamps are being drained, and forests are being leveled to make way for building more homes for urban families. One species is replacing another by making land habitable that had been inhospitable to humans.

Paul says Christians are made into a "new creation." The word in the Greek is *ktisis*, which comes from the verb *ktidzo*, meaning "to make habitable" or "to people." Prior to our regeneration we were a collection of spiritual bogs and swamps, completely uninhabitable by holiness. It is possible Paul is talking about such hostile, unregenerate people when he tells the Corinthians, "I have fought with beasts at Ephesus" (1 Cor. 15:32).

Yet when we receive Christ, the landscape is changed forever. The bogs are filled in, the swamps are drained, and we become inhabitable—and the Holy Spirit comes to dwell in us (John 14:17). In this case, driving out the former inhabitants of the bogs and swamps of our life is a positive thing. The Holy Spirit will *influence* an unbeliever, but He will not *indwell* him. It takes much more than an environmental study to make us inhabitable by the Spirit of God. It takes the work of regeneration.

We are new

The Greeks had two words for *new*. One was *neos*, which means "new in time." This word was used to indicate "new wine" in the sense of "freshly made" (Matt. 9:17; Mark 2:22). The other word was *kainos*, which is used in 2 Corinthians 5:17. *Kainos* means "new in substance."

In other words, these particular molecules have never been arranged this way before. It is unprecedented, original.

When God created a new species of man through regeneration, it was something that the world had never seen before. Not even Adam was the same as regenerated man. Adam and Eve had been created to have fellowship with God, but not to be indwelt by Him. Thus we could say there have been three species of man (spiritually speaking). In the beginning there was the original species, Adam and Eve, who were sinless and pure. After the Fall there was the sinful species, all of mankind, who was inhabitable and fit only for wild beasts. Then, when redeemed through Jesus, some members of this sinful species became yet a third species: a special people indwelt by the Spirit of God (1 Pet. 2:9). We became a totally new man. This was no makeover; it was a transformation. By God's grace we are totally new.

We are purebred

A friend of mine said that he wanted to name his family's new dog "Heinz" because it looked liked it had 57 different breeds in it. There is certainly nothing wrong with dogs who have a mixed pedigree; sometimes they make the nicest pets. But God isn't interested in making us pets; He is interested in making us new creatures. When it comes to our spiritual pedigree, God goes only for purebreds.

Some Bible students believe that man has an "old nature," which represents our character before we receive Christ as our Savior. They call it the "old man" and think that when we receive Christ, we receive a new nature and the two natures, "old man" and "new man," share our body, battling it out on a daily basis. They think whichever man is "fed" the most dominates our character.

But I don't see that taught in the Bible at all. Paul says in Romans 6:6, "Knowing this, that our old man was crucified with Him, that the body of sin might be done away with, that we should no longer be slaves of sin." What happened to our old man when we were saved? He was crucified. No one comes down from a cross alive. Our old man was destroyed. Second Corinthians 5:17 says, "old things have passed away." The word for "passed away" is *parerchomai*, which means "to be removed" or "perish." There is no "coexistence" agreement. Our old nature is not sharing our body with the new nature. The old nature is gone for good.

Where the confusion comes, however, is that we still have many of the habits and appetites that were developed under the old nature. This is what Paul is talking about when he says, "Do not lie to one another, since you have put off the old man with his deeds, and have put on the new man who is renewed in knowledge according to the image of Him who created him" (Col. 3:9–10). Notice that Paul says, "you have put off the old man"; therefore, don't do those things which you did before you became a Christian. When we do those things we learned under the old man, we operate under the influence of the flesh instead of under the influence of the Spirit. There's no question about our nature here: we are new creatures and have a new nature. It's the old habits of our flesh that trip us up.

The next time you cave into sin, don't blame your old nature. Your old nature is in the grave. The old man is gone. Blame the flesh and your inability to control your flesh. You grieve the Spirit when you sin because instead of living in the Spirit, you live in the desires of the flesh.

A new identity

In the United States, as well as in many other countries, there is a serious problem with organized crime. While law enforcement agencies are seeing more successes now than ever before in wiping out organized crime, it still dramatically makes its presence known in society. One of the country's most powerful weapons against crime is the informant, someone who will go to the police or FBI and tell them all they know about a crime syndicate in exchange for immunity from prosecution. This action sometimes requires one additional step—assuming a new name and a new identity to hide from the crime bosses forever. Informants enter the Witness Protection Program, in which law enforcement authorities place an informant in a new location, with a new name and identity in order to give that person a fresh start in life.

A new name, a new identity and a new location, however, do not materially change anything. The change is all on the surface, for others to see. God doesn't work that way. When God gives you a new identity, He begins to work from the inside. He gives you a new heart, a new spirit, a new life. You are made new from the inside out. He said to Israel, "I will give you a new heart and put a new spirit within you; I will take the heart of stone out of your flesh and give you a heart of flesh. I will put My Spirit within you and cause you to walk in My statutes, and you will keep My judgments and do them" (Ezk. 36:26). If that was true of hard-hearted Israel in the Old Testament, think of how true it can be for you today.

When you become a new creature in Christ, inhabitable by the Holy Spirit, you are a new kind of creation, unprecedented, never before seen. The old creature you once were, all of what you were, every part of what your nature used to be, perished. Your old man died. He was crucified with Christ at the cross of Calvary (Gal. 2:20). You have a new life, with a new identity to go along with your new nature. It's that new identity we will focus on in the next chapter.

---

1 *Church* here means all people — past, present and future — who have received Christ as their Savior and are now part of God's family. They belong to the Lord and experience all the blessings of this personal relationship. This is different from the local church, which contains both saved and unsaved individuals.

2 Joseph Bayly, *The View From a Hearse* (Elgin, Ill.: David C. Cook Publishing, 1969), p. 13.

3 Ann Landers, "Aim at profits to clean up trashy TV," *Indianapolis Star*, April 16, 1995.

4 Mona Charen, "Neglecting the story on religion," *Indianapolis Star*, May 10, 1995.

Chapter 6

Belonging: The Expression of a New Identity

One of my responsibilities as General Director for Back to the Bible is to represent the ministry at various functions. When I arrive I'm usually given a tag that gives my name and the name of the ministry I represent. This tag not only expresses my identity, but it becomes my entrance pass to meetings. It both identifies me and legitimizes me. It tells everyone that "I belong."

When you become a new creature in Christ Jesus, when you are born again, born from above, born to live forever by God's grace, you receive a new identity. This identity both tells the world who you are and verifies that you belong to the family of God.

Belonging to the world

Before you became a new creation in Christ, you belonged to the world. This was a very unsatisfying experience. In the world everyone is so concerned about getting *their* needs met they don't have time to think about anyone else. The world's view is clearly illustrated in the story of the two hikers who confronted a giant bear. One of the men took off his boots, pulled out a pair of tennis shoes and began putting them on.

"What are you doing?" questioned his companion. "We can't outrun that bear, even with jogging shoes."

"Who cares about the bear?" the first hiker replied. "All I have to worry about is outrunning you."

Selfishness and self-centeredness are a part of belonging to the world. The world's underlying philosophy is represented in the book *Looking Out for #1*. But the world's view is also extremely shallow. People are interested in exterior things, such as youth, beauty and materialism. Nothing in belonging to the world actually gets down to that deep "hole in the soul" that causes people to feel so empty. Our identity in the world is based on such things as:

Our name

The right name can open doors to all kinds of opportunities. Social functions are often simply occasions to make contact with the "right names." You need to belong to the right clubs, be invited to the right parties, even belong to the right church. Many people spend a great deal of money and expend an even greater amount of energy "to make a name for themselves."

When Ptolemy, a second century B.C. Greek astronomer and mathematician, decided to build the mammoth lighthouse at Pharos, he asked Sostratus to design the structure. Later it became one of the Seven Wonders of the world. Ptolemy, however, insisted that the lighthouse carry an inscription bearing his name as a personal memorial. Sostratus, however, didn't think the king should get all the credit, so he put "Ptolemy" on the front of the lighthouse in a thick plaster that would be eye-catching at first, but later would be worn away by the wind and waves. Secretly he carved his own name in the granite underneath. For years the sea dashed against Ptolemy's inscription and gradually eroded it. Though it lasted the lifetime of the monarch, it finally was obliterated, leaving the name "Sostratus" standing in bold relief. Again the lesson of time and eternity is illustrated. Worldly fame often disappears before the relentless tides of time, but eternity's fame endures forever. Each day we are faced with time and eternity choices. Living for the world is a choice for time; living for God is a choice for eternity.

The late British author and noted Christian Malcolm Muggeridge had a balanced perspective on this. He said,

> I may, I suppose, regard myself, or pass for being, a relatively successful man. People occasionally stare at me in the streets—that's fame. I can fairly easily earn enough to qualify for admission to the higher slopes of the Internal Revenue—that's success. Furnished with money and little fame, even the elderly, if they care to, may partake of trendy diversions—that's pleasure. It might happen once in a while that something I said or wrote was sufficiently heeded for me to persuade myself that it represented a serious impact on our time—that's fulfillment. Yet I say to you and I beg you to believe me: multiply these tiny triumphs by a million, add them

all together, and they are nothing less than nothing; a positive impediment measured against one draught of that living water Christ offers to the spiritually thirsty, irrespective of who or what they are. [1]

When all is said and done, fame is as fleeting as a soap bubble and just as fulfilling. As world heavyweight champion Muhammad Ali once said, "I had the world, and it wasn't nothin'."

Our personal appearance

Western society is in love with youth and beauty. Diets, exercise, face-lifts and shopping trips are a necessary part of the ritual if you want the world to beat a path to your door. It's not surprising that the New York fashion industry is valued at $22 billion. Americans spent $129 billion on clothing in 1993. New York City alone houses 5,100 designer showrooms or fashion houses.[2]

In the United States each year, we buy 1,484 tubes of lipstick (at a cost of $4,566), 913 bottles of nail polish ($2,055), 1,324 mascaras, eye shadows and eyeliners ($6,849) and 2,055 jars of skin care products ($12,785) *every minute*. That's $1,581,300 an hour. Today, beauty product marketing represents an almost $17 billion-per-year business in the U.S., with an annual expenditure per person of about $70, compared with $40 million in 1914, when per capita spending ran about 40 cents each year.[3]

Even dental hygiene is getting into the trend. It used to be if you didn't have a "movie star smile," you were limited to repairing an offending tooth by crowns or braces. Today, dentists trained in cosmetic procedures can change a tooth's shape, replace missing teeth, cover badly stained ones and close wide gaps.[4] For people who set a high priority on their personal appearance, the sometimes exorbitant cost of these procedures don't seem to stop them. After all, it's either join the mad throng or get trampled from behind. That's the way it is when you belong to the world.

Belonging to Christ

Our identity in the world hinged on external qualifications, things like fame and physical appearance. Does this change when we become a Christian? Absolutely. The key word for our Christian identity is *relationship*. Our identity in Christ is not based on things; it's based on our affiliation. This has a tremendous impact on who we are. In order to understand our identity, we need to understand how we are related to Christ.

A family relationship

We will take a closer look at what it means to be a son or daughter in God's family in chapter 8. The truth I want to emphasize here is that it is a family relationship based on love. The apostle John writes, "Behold what manner of love the Father has bestowed on us, that we should be called children of God!" (1 John 3:1). God the Father had no need for a family. He and God the Son and God the Holy Spirit constituted their own family. From their own experience, however, they knew how wonderful and fulfilling a family relationship could be. God wanted others to have this same experience. Out of totally unselfish love, God created Adam and Eve and gave them the opportunity to be a family also. He told them to "be fruitful and multiply" (Gen. 1:28).

Sin, of course, did serious damage to all of our relationships, including our family relationship. Tim Timmons and Stephen Arterburn report that sociologists tell us "the most dangerous place to be on a Friday night is not on the street but in many homes across the land. Family violence today is occurring in epidemic proportions. Among families, marriages are not working, parenting is less effective, and individuals are obsessed with self-satisfaction. Sociological time bombs are exploding in our homes."[5] Without Christ, family life can never be the wonderful experience God intended it to be.

So again out of love, God stepped into the lives of His creation and redeemed them. Probably the best-known verse in the Bible says, "For God so loved the world that He gave His only begotten Son, that whoever believes in Him should not perish but have everlasting life" (John 3:16). It was Christ's blood that broke down the walls of separation between people (Eph. 2:14) and made us one large family—not the family of man, but the family of God. All who are born again, whether male or female, black or white, from the Northern or Southern hemisphere, are a part of God's family.

An exclusive relationship

Some people argue that everyone is a "child of God." In fact, they become quite upset at the "narrow-mindedness" and "bigotry" that Christians demonstrate in this area. They protest, "What about the sincere Hindu or Buddhist? Will God condemn them because they aren't Christians?" No, He will not condemn them because they aren't Christians. But He *will* condemn them because they haven't lived up to His standards of righteousness. Paul says in Romans 1:20-25,

> For since the creation of the world His invisible attributes are clearly seen, being understood by the things that are made, even His eternal power and Godhead, so that they are without excuse, because, although they knew God, they did not glorify Him as God, nor were thankful, but became futile in their thoughts, and their foolish hearts were darkened. Professing to be wise, they became fools, and changed the glory of the incorruptible God into an image made like corruptible man—and birds and four-footed animals and creeping things. Therefore God also gave them up to uncleanness, in the lusts of their hearts, to dishonor their bodies among themselves, who exchanged the truth of God for the lie, and worshiped and served the creature rather than the Creator, who is blessed forever. Amen.

Man's natural response is to reject God. It is only by His grace that any of us choose to accept His offer of mercy through Christ. Hindus, Buddhists, Muslims, animists, spir-

it worshipers and even many who call themselves
Christians have rejected the righteous standard of God and
have attempted to establish their own righteousness. They
have failed, and failure in this arena means we fail to discover the joy of belonging to God.

Furthermore, Jesus Himself drew the boundaries. He
said in John 14:6, "I am the way, the truth, and the life. No
one comes to the Father except through Me." He also
warned, "Many will say to Me in that day, 'Lord, Lord, have
we not prophesied in Your name, cast out demons in Your
name, and done many wonders in Your name?' And then I
will declare to them, 'I never knew you; depart from Me,
you who practice lawlessness!'" (Matt. 7:22-23).

Belonging to God's family puts us in very special company. For only "as many as received Him, to them He gave
the right to become children of God, even to those who
believe in His name: who were born, not of blood, nor of
the will of the flesh, nor of the will of man, but of God"
(John 1:12-13). We didn't establish this exclusive relationship with God, but we can thank Him for it.

A satisfying relationship

Psychologists have discovered a quirk in human nature
called the "Twenty Percent Rule." When questioned, people at all financial levels said they would be satisfied if they
could make about 20 percent more than they currently
earned. There is another twist in our human nature, however, that undermines this belief. It's called "adaptation."
You may have noticed that when you put your watch on for

the first time, you can feel it on your wrist. In a short time, however, you adapt to the sensation and no longer notice it. The same is true mentally. After each pay increase, we adapt to our new financial level and that old longing for "20 percent more" returns. It's a vicious cycle. In essence, we are doomed never to be satisfied with material possessions.

However, Jesus does truly satisfy. King David knew this even though he lived in Old Testament times. He wrote, "The LORD is my shepherd; I shall not want" (Ps. 23:1). In other words, "The Lord is my shepherd; therefore I will be satisfied." David then wrote five more verses of Psalm 23, sharing how his Shepherd (whom we know as Jesus) can satisfy.

David knew that the Shepherd could meet our physical needs: green meadows and quiet waters (v. 2). The apostle Paul said, "And my God shall supply all your need according to His riches in glory by Christ Jesus" (Phil. 4:19).

The Shepherd meets our spiritual needs too: He restores our souls and leads us in the paths of righteousness (v. 3). The Hebrew word translated "restore" (*shuwb*) literally means "to put back on one's feet. It was used to describe what a shepherd did when he found one of his sheep on its back and unable to get up. Such a position was indefensible and fatal unless the sheep was found and "restored." Our Shepherd restored us when we were helpless. Ephesians 2:1 says, "And you He made alive, who were dead in trespasses and sins." No one is more helpless than a dead person. He can do nothing to restore himself. Likewise, we were spiritually stillborn, born dead in our sins. It took Jesus to put us back on our feet.

Our Shepherd also keeps us restored, or as David says, "He leads me in the paths of righteousness" (v. 3). Jesus promised that He would send "the Helper, the Holy Spirit, whom the Father will send in My name, He will teach you all things, and bring to your remembrance all things that I said to you" (John 14:26). Through the Holy Spirit's ministry not only are we restored, but we are maintained.

In addition, the Shepherd meets our emotional needs. David declares, "Yea, though I walk through the valley of the shadow of death, I will fear no evil; for You are with me; Your rod and Your staff, they comfort me" (v. 4). Paul calls Him the "God of all comfort, who comforts us in all our tribulation" (2 Cor. 1:3-4).

Then, finally, our Shepherd meets our eternal needs. David is assured that he "will dwell in the house of the LORD forever" (v. 6). Paul tells us that when the Lord returns, "We who are alive and remain shall be caught up together with them in the clouds to meet the Lord in the air. And thus we shall always be with the Lord" (1 Thess. 4:17).

When we belong to Christ, we can truly be satisfied. He leaves no area unguarded; He leaves no need unmet.

A growing relationship

Our relationship with the Lord is never at a standstill. We are either moving forward or slipping backwards. Peter urges us to "grow in the grace and knowledge of our Lord and Savior Jesus Christ" (2 Pet. 3:18). Don't be afraid of growing; be afraid of standing still.

Growth is possible for everyone who knows Christ. In May 1855, an 18-year-old boy went to the deacons of a church in Boston. He had been raised in a Unitarian church and knew almost nothing about the Gospel. Only a month before he had surrendered his life to Jesus. Now he wanted to join the church. The deacons were upset. Not only was he ignorant of much of the Gospel, but he was also uneducated and uncouth. They finally decided to put him on a year-long course of instruction. At the end of the year, however, it didn't seem to have done much good. Not knowing what else to do, the deacons finally accepted him as a member—but they were sure he would never amount to much. That boy was D. L. Moody.

Remember, too, that the road to growth is not necessarily a fast one. That may be a plus. Huge plants and trees grow quickly in tropical rain forests. Sometimes they seem to sprout almost overnight. But these trees have soft wood and they fall victim to insects and diseases that drastically shorten their life span. On the other hand, in the rugged mountains of the north, growth is slow. Plants and trees endure high winds, ice storms and intense cold. But they grow strong and tough with knotty, hard wood. It's not always how fast we're moving that counts; it's whether or not we're moving in the right direction. Be patient and don't give up on yourself. With time and trials you will grow strong.

We never reach a point where no more growth is possible. It's sad to see Christians who once were active in Bible study, witnessing and the work of Christ's church suddenly decide to "coast" during their latter years. I've read of a monument high in the Alps raised in honor of a faithful guide who perished while ascending a peak to rescue a stranded tourist. Inscribed on that memorial stone are these words: HE DIED CLIMBING. A maturing, growing Christian should have the same kind of attitude, right to the end of his life.

Who are we?

When we think of who we are as members of God's family, we can sum it up in three words: WE ARE SPECIAL. Our significance comes not from the world but from our relationship with God through His Son. God created us special, but our specialness was dealt a death blow in the Garden of Eden. Our relationship with God was severed. We wanted to be on our own, and God permitted it because of our sin. But at the cross of Calvary Jesus restored that relationship. Who we were before we trusted Christ as Savior is not at all who we are now. As a Christian, I'm not all that I ought to be. I'm not all that I want to be. Perhaps I'm not all that I can be. But, thank God, I'm not all that I used to be.

Who are we in Christ? We are special people, peculiar to Him. We have a restored relationship with God the Father; He is our provider and protector. We have a restored relationship with God the Son; He is our Lord and Savior. We have a restored relationship with God the Spirit; He is our mentor and teacher. If you aren't special, Christian, who is?

1 Malcolm Muggeridge, *Jesus Rediscovered* (Garden City, N.Y.: Doubleday, 1969), p. 61.

2 "Outlook," *U.S. News & World Report*, March 6, 1995, p. 18.

3 Debra Evans, "Best and the Beauty," *Focus on the Family*, Colorado Springs, 1993, p. 42.

4 Veronique De Turenne, "Cosmetic dentistry enables masses to sport star smiles," *Lincoln Journal Star*, October 9, 1995, p. D-2.

5 Tim Timmons and Stephen Arterburn, *Hooked on Life* (Nashville, Tenn.: Nelson, 1989), p. 34.

Chapter 7

Belonging: The Call to Sainthood

Do you know any saints? That term is used loosely today. According to one source, there have been four American saints. The first is Elizabeth Ann Seton (1774-1821), who was known as the mother of the U.S. parochial school system. The other American saints (although not native-born) include Frances Cabrini, John Neumann and Rose Philippine Duchesne.[1] These individuals came to the status of sainthood by being canonized. Canonization occurs after a person's life has been closely examined by a committee of the Roman Catholic church. If that committee judges the person worthy, he or she is declared "blessed."[2] If further investigation produces proof of two miracles associated with the person, he or she may be canonized.[3]

While this is how one church determines sainthood, the Bible teaches something very different. God's Scriptures indicate that when we receive Christ as our Savior, we automatically become a part of that special group called saints. There is no beatification or canonization necessary. Sainthood is not based on how good we are but on how gracious God is. Paul addressed the carnal Christians at Corinth as well as the godly Christians at Philippi as saints.

Like salvation, saintliness is not a process but a position. We are not saints by our merits but because we belong to God's family.

Being a saint, however, is not just a position to hold but a calling to fulfill. Paul addressed the Roman believers as those "who are in Rome, beloved of God, *called to be saints*" (Rom. 1:7, italics mine). Again in 1 Corinthians 1:2 Paul says, "To the church of God which is at Corinth, to those who are sanctified in Christ Jesus, *called to be saints*" (italics mine).

While our position as "saint" is not determined by works, we still have a responsibility to live saintly lives. Our calling as saints is reflected in:

A passionate life

Some time ago I saw a bumper sticker that would have been appropriate over the entrances to many churches. It said, "Complacency is America's greatest problem . . . but who cares!" Americans are rich (compared with the rest of the world) and in want of nothing. The American church has little or no persecution and finds it difficult to identify with those who do. In effect, many people in the church have become fat and complacent. We have fallen into one of Satan's most subtle deceptions—a sleepy coexistence with the world.

But Jude, a half brother of the Lord Jesus Christ, wrote, "Beloved . . . I found it necessary to write to you exhorting you to contend earnestly for the faith which was once for all delivered to the saints" (Jude 1:3). The expression "contend earnestly" is an athletic term associated with wrestling. An outfielder might doze off in right field if the opposing team never hits the baseball his way, but wrestling requires the utmost effort at every moment.

Some might say, "Why all the concern? A lot of churches still preach the Gospel." Gratefully, this is true—but the tide is changing. The world is becoming desensitized to the sinful practices that are so prevalent in our society. Like frogs in a kettle in which the temperature is slowing rising, we stand in danger of being boiled to death.[4] As an illustration of this tendency, consider the following letter, entitled "Witches have feelings, too." It was sent to advice columnist Ann Landers and is a clear indication of where the American culture is headed:

Dear Ann: I am writing in regard to your answer to "J. F. in Philadelphia," whose "Aunt Di" was behaving in an ill-tempered and childish manner. The first sentence of your response was "Aunt Di sounds like a witch."

As a minister of the Old Religion, whose priests and priestesses call themselves witches, I take issue with your derogatory characterization of witches. It was not only unfair but inaccurate.

While it is true that the word "witch" has the connotation of an evil person, that stereotype is no more accurate than the long outdated stereotype of blacks or Jews. Yet, 50 years ago, such characterizations were common in our language.

It took sensitivity and understanding of the harm done by such stereotyping before the public stopped using those characterizations. And because blacks and Jews were vocal about their objections to such stereotyping, they were able to educate the public.

Witches are members of a religion that predates Christianity in Europe. We worship both a male deity and a female deity. We strive to understand the connections between all things, and we respect and honor nature as the expression of divinity and of those connections. To continue to equate us in the popular mind with evil and unkind behavior does us a grave disservice and perpetuates an unfair and false image.

I know from many years of reading your column that you are not a prejudiced person. Please educate yourself on the subject of witches and refrain from continuing a damaging stereotype.[5]

Ann's response to this letter? She apologized! Those issues and practices that are clearly forbidden in Scripture (witchcraft, homosexuality, abortion, etc.) are today frequently equated with race and/or color and have become not a matter of right or wrong but of civil rights.

Now more than ever we who are the true saints in the scriptural sense need to take a passionate stand for the clear teachings of the Bible and against the increasingly godless practices of our society. Saints must wake up and defend the truth.

A purified life

Sensuality also has become a genuine threat to God's saints. R. Kent Hughes reported, "*Christianity Today* surveyed a thousand of its subscribers and found that 23 percent admitted having extramarital intercourse; 45 percent indicated they had done something they themselves deemed sexually inappropriate. One in four Christian men are unfaithful and nearly one half have behaved unbecomingly."[6] When you remember that these subscribers are likely to be "conservative" Christians, the magnitude of the problem is enhanced.

Paul warned, "But fornication and all uncleanness or covetousness, let it not even be named among you, as is fitting for saints; neither filthiness, nor foolish talking, nor coarse jesting, which are not fitting, but rather giving of thanks" (Eph. 5:3–4).

The apostle says we need to watch not only our actions but also our mouths. We are daily inundated with the foul language of television, rock songs and the workplace. As a result, it's easy to slip into using language that is inappropriate for Christians. Even if it's not filthy, it can be foolish. Paul is not condemning honest humor (cf. Prov. 17:22); he is rebuking those who engage in idle conversation that edifies no one.

Perhaps the most common form of foolish talk is gossip. Author Max Lucado shares a story about a woman wounded by gossip:

I once knew an extremely courageous lady. She

was courageous for several reasons. For one thing, she was waging an uphill battle against alcoholism. For another, she was doing all she could to restore her relationship with God. It's tough to start over. It's even tougher to start over when people won't let you.

She chose a small church to attend, a church where she knew many members. She thought she'd be received there. One Sunday she parked her car near the church building and got out. As she walked toward the front door, she overheard two ladies talking nearby. The stinging words were not meant for her ears, but she heard them anyway.

"How long is that alcoholic going to hang around here?"

She turned and went back to the car. She never entered another church building until she died. Those ladies meant no harm, yet seemingly painless gossip did irreparable damage.[7]

The injury done by careless tongues as well as careless lives is incalculable. The only solution is to make sure we are guilty of neither. How do you do that? Politely excuse yourself if your coffee break mates become foul or foolish. Consider talking to your supervisor if your work environment is polluted with verbal garbage. Switch channels or turn the TV off if a program uses offensive language. Pray for protection from any influence that would impinge upon your purity.

A peaceful life

When Jesus saves saints He creates peace. First, He creates peace between God and us. Before our salvation we were at war with God. As His enemies, we were rebels against righteousness. But once we were justified by faith, Jesus became our peace treaty with God. Now we have peace with God through the Lord Jesus Christ (Rom. 5:1). But more than that, Jesus makes peace between us and others as well. Speaking of the differences between Jews and Gentiles and how those differences were bridged by the blood of Christ, Paul said, "For He Himself is our peace, who has made both one, and has broken down the middle wall of partition between us; having abolished in His flesh the enmity . . . to create in Himself one new man from the two, thus making peace" (Eph. 2:14–15).

If Christ has made peace between saints, why is there so little peace in the church? The late J. Vernon McGee spent many years in ministry. He summed up his opinion of the church in the following poem:

Like a halting caravan, moves the church of Christ;

We are feebly faltering toward our timid tryst.

We are all divided, many bodies we,

Kept apart by doctrine and lack of charity.

Careful, Christian pilgrims! Walk in doubt and fear,

With the cross of Jesus, bringing up the rear.

The bickering and quarreling between churches and church members is a sad commentary on the lives of the saints. But this isn't anything new. Even to the loving church at Philippi, Paul had to say, "I implore Euodia and I implore Syntyche to be of the same mind in the Lord" (Phil. 4:2). It's no wonder that Paul addressed believers ten times with the greeting "grace to you and *peace*" (as did Peter in 1 Peter 1:2 and John in Revelation 1:4, italics mine). Of course the primary thought of these writers was peace with God. But this peace extends farther than that. When we are at peace with God, we can be at peace with ourselves. When we are at peace with ourselves, we can be at peace with others.

It is unfortunate that some saints go no farther than peace with God. Instead of allowing that peace to flow through them and project to others, they continue their cantankerous lifestyle learned in their carnal days. It is understandable why Jesus said, "Blessed are the peacemakers, for they shall be called sons of God" (Matt. 5:9).

As we war with and wound one another, the enemy gleefully cheers from the sidelines. We need individuals in the church who will act as did Lord Horatio Nelson. Prior to the famous battle of Trafalger, commander Lord Nelson discovered that two of his top officers were not on speaking terms. He ordered them to the deck and pointed off to the French fleet. "There," said the admiral, "is the enemy."

Paul exhorts Christians everywhere, "If it is possible, as much as depends on you, live peaceably with all men" (Rom. 12:18). If the church is ever going to reach the world with the Gospel of peace, it first must be at peace with itself.

A prayerful life

Prayer is the lifeline of the saint. The effective Christian life can no more be lived without prayer than a deep sea diver can live without his oxygen tank. Jesus recognized that. No matter how busy He was, no matter how pressured the day, He always took time to pray. Mark tells us that after ministering to 5,000 men, Jesus "departed to the mountain to pray" (Mark 6:46). On another occasion, after spending a late night ministering to those in need, Jesus, "having risen a long while before daylight . . . went out and departed to a solitary place; and there He prayed" (1:35). Like Jesus, great church leaders recognized the importance of prayer. Martin Luther said, "If I should neglect prayer but a single day, I should lose a great deal of the fire of faith."[8]

Why do saintly people emphasize prayer? Because they know the influence that prayer has in heaven. The apostle John was taken up into heaven (Rev. 4:1), where he saw how God deals with the prayers of the saints. In Revelation 8:3-4, John says, "Then another angel, having a golden censer, came and stood at the altar. And he was given much incense, that he should offer it with the prayers of all the saints upon the golden altar which was before the throne. And the smoke of the incense, with the prayers of the saints, ascended before God from the angel's hand."

The prayers of the saints are brought before the throne of God and are made even more pleasing to Him by the addition of incense (an aromatic mixture used in worship). In fact, John said "much incense" was added. The odor of our prayers fills the temple of God and gives Him pleasure.

One study showed that busy executives spend nearly 60 hours a year on the telephone waiting on hold. How wonderful it is to know that God is always available. As soon as we begin to pray, those prayers are brought before God's symbol of authority (the throne) for His attention and for His pleasure.

A privileged life

In the popular television show "The Lifestyles of the Rich and Famous," Robin Leach shows viewers the homes, possessions and activities of privileged people. Some are featured because of the money they have earned; others are privileged by the social class into which they were born. All of them, however, are set apart from the rank and file by their wealth.

God tells us that saints are also privileged. We who have come into a saving relationship with Christ have something no one has ever had before. Colossians 1:26 says we have "the mystery which has been hidden from ages and from generations, but now has been revealed to His saints." This doesn't mean no one knows about it. Indeed, it is a "revealed" mystery. What the Old Testament saints didn't completely understand—how God was going to provide the atonement for man's sin—is now obvious. But it is obvious only to those who believe. The apostle Paul says, "For the message of the cross is foolishness to those who are perishing, but to us who are being saved it is the power of God" (1 Cor. 1:18).

As saints, we have a privilege that far exceeds material wealth or earthly position. We have a spiritual knowledge and a personal experience that will last for all of eternity.

A persecuted life

God never promised His people an easy life. Some claim that the church grows only when it's watered by the blood of its martyrs. While few of us in the United States have found it necessary to give our life for our faith, that's certainly not been true of Christians in the past. An article in *Biblical Archaeology Review* reports the finding of a mass burial cave containing the remains of several hundred Christians killed in the Persian conquest of Jerusalem in 614 A.D. This is only one of at least 35 sites where bodies from this massacre were buried. Estimates of the total number of Christians killed range from 37,585 to 65,262.[9] These men, women and children perished because they were saints, followers of Jesus Christ.

Even if your sacrifices are not as extreme, you should expect some repercussions if you are living a committed Christian life. Some Christians have lost job promotions because of their stand for Christ; others have been falsely accused of a variety of offenses; and yet others have been the object of malicious humor because they have chosen to express their faith openly.

Life can surely hurt and grieve us. The apostle Peter says, "In this you greatly rejoice, though now for a little while, if need be, you have been grieved by various trials"

(1 Pet. 1:6). Christians' hearts are not unbreakable, but they are undefeatable. In the midst of pain and sorrow, we have the joy of knowing that better days are coming. The victory is ours! Jesus is coming—not only to take us home but to set right all the wrongs that have been done.

In the meantime, Jesus reminds us, "And do not fear those who kill the body but cannot kill the soul. But rather fear Him who is able to destroy both soul and body in hell" (Matt. 10:28). When we fear God, we don't have to fear man.

Welcome to sainthood

While there aren't as many saints in the United States as we would like there to be, there are certainly more than four. If you have received Christ as your Savior, you are one of them. There are millions of us. That doesn't mean we're perfect; it doesn't mean we're able to perform miracles. It simply means that we have been restored to the joy of belonging to Christ.

If you thought a saint was someone who lived a good life and is now dead, think again. The Bible says a saint is some-one who was dead and is now alive in Christ, living a good life. Each day the ranks of the saints grows, even though some of our ranks are graduated to heaven. If you've only recently joined the family of God, welcome to sainthood!

[1] "Outlook," *U. S. News & World Report*, September 11, 1995, p. 8.

[2] This is called "beatification."

[3] Or "officially recognized."

[4] George Barna uses this illustration in his book *The Frog in the Kettle*. Because of the circulatory system of frogs, if one is placed in a kettle of water over a flame, it will not notice the rise in temperature of the water. Even though the temperature eventually will reach the boiling point (which naturally kills the frog), it will not attempt to escape.

[5] Ann Landers, "Witches have feelings, too," *Lincoln Journal Star*, February 20, 1996, p. A-8.

[6] R. Kent Hughes, *Disciplines of a Godly Man* (Wheaton, Ill.: Crossway Books, 1991), p. 24.

[7] Max Lucado, *On the Anvil* (Wheaton, Ill.: Tyndale House, 1985), p. 119.

[8] *Tabletalk*, Vol. 11, No. 1, February 1987.

[9] Ronny Reich, "God Knows Their Names," *Biblical Archaeology Review*, March/April 1996, pp. 26-33, 60.

Chapter 8

Belonging: The Privileges of Sonship

The United States is the most privileged nation in history. While we have only about 6% of the world's population, we have

50% of the world's wealth

63% of the world's manufactured goods

29% of the world's railroads

58% of the world's automobiles

44% of the world's trucks

56% of the world's telephones

43% of the world's radios

35% of the world's electrical output

26% of the world's steel

29% of the world's petroleum

22% of the world's coal[1]

Only one other position could be more privileged— being a part of God's family. When we receive Christ, we become sons and daughters of the King of the universe, with all the privileges that such a relationship involves.

Sonship (meaning both sons and daughters) includes the privileges of adoption, freedom and discipline.

The privilege of adoption

Galatians 4:4-5 says, "But when the fullness of the time had come, God sent forth His Son, born of a woman, born under the law, to redeem those who were under the law, that we might receive the adoption as sons." The word translated "redeem" in this verse is *agorazo*. It literally means "to buy out of the marketplace" (the word *agora* means "marketplace"). This, however, is not adoption. It is only the first step toward adoption. We are redeemed, Paul says, that we *might receive* the adoption. God can't adopt into His family a person who is a slave to sin. Such a person simply wouldn't fit in. It would be like trying to get a school of fish to adopt a cat. It would be impossible. So God first redeems us—He buys us out of our enslavement and gives us a new nature.

Having redeemed us, God then adopts us, but unlike most adoptions today, He does not adopt us as children. The word *adoption* in the New Testament means "being placed as an adult son." The instant we are born into the family, God adopts us and gives us the position of an adult. A baby cannot walk, speak, make decisions or draw upon the family wealth. But the believer can do all of these the instant he is born again. When we are adopted, we are given not only the position but also the privileges of an adult son or daughter. We don't have to wait until we have been in God's family for years before we can draw on His riches. Immediately we can begin to:

Pray

While the years may bring a greater ease and eloquence to our praying, they will add nothing to our effectiveness. From the moment we are received into God's family, we have the privilege of intimate communion with God just as surely as those who have been adopted for a much longer time. In fact, some of the most delightful prayers I've heard have been uttered by more recent members of God's family. They are fresh and unstilted. These new sons and daughters haven't had time to learn all the "prayeraphrases" that older Christians have. They just talk to God as a respected Friend. They don't even know how to switch to that "praying tone" that many older Christians have assumed. Instead, they talk to God in real terms, and I think God finds that refreshing.

Tap into God's power

When applying for a line of credit, a person is often required to wait weeks until all his credit references are checked and the paperwork is processed. But not with God! The moment we are adopted as His children we can plug into His power to experience victory over sin, triumph over trials and much, much more. To use an expression from the computer world, it is truly "plug and play." God not only gives us opportunities to act like an adult, He gives us the power.

The power of God is the power by which we live the Christian life. As adult sons you and I have certain rights and privileges, but we have certain responsibilities as well. We are to walk worthy of our standing in Christ (Eph. 4:1), but we cannot do that in our own power. When we try, we fail. But the Holy Spirit dwells in us to energize us with the power necessary to accomplish all things that please God. When we tap into His power, we are victorious in warring against our old enemy, the devil (Gal. 5:16), and we are successful in serving our Savior (Acts 1:8) and in worshiping Him (John 4:24). In fact, we can do the will of God only in the power of Christ, which He gives us through the indwelling Holy Spirit (Phil. 4:13; John 15:5).

Evangelize

We often excuse our lack of zeal for evangelism by claiming, "I haven't been a Christian long enough to tell others about Christ." But Christ says, "You shall receive power when the Holy Spirit has come upon you; and you shall be witnesses to Me in Jerusalem, and in all Judea and Samaria, and to the end of the earth" (Acts 1:8). Notice that this power comes with the Holy Spirit. We receive the Holy Spirit when we are redeemed and adopted into God's family (Gal. 3:3). One reason we are so quickly empowered by God is so that we immediately may be witnesses for Him. You don't have to wait until you finish seminary or attend a weekend seminar on witnessing. The time for evangelism is right now, and the opportunities are real now.

But you argue, "I won't be polished in what I say. In fact, I won't know what to say." That's true, but is it relevant? When Jesus spoke to the Samaritan woman at the well (John 4:7-26) and she believed, "the woman then left her waterpot, went her way into the city, and said to the men, 'Come, see a Man who told me all things that I ever did. Could this be the Christ?'" (vv. 28-29). Her words were not particularly eloquent. She had never watched a video on how to win others to Christ. She had good news and needed to share it. She didn't wait; instead, she laid hold of her adult status in God's family and began to share with others what Christ had done for her.

Remember when you were a child? The wait for Christmas seemed interminable; the day that you would be old enough to get a driver's license appeared frustratingly distant; the age at which you could legally do the things you wanted seemed to crawl toward you at a snail's pace. How different with salvation. When you were adopted into God's family, you began to enjoy the privileges of adulthood instantly.

The privilege of freedom

Historians have estimated that there were 60 million slaves in the Roman Empire. In fact, slaves far outnumbered freemen. Unfortunately, the same is true today when we look at the spiritual world. The majority of the world lives in bondage to sin. They are slaves to the lusts of their flesh, the desires of their eyes and the pride of their life (1 John 2:16). Slavery was a cruel institution. A slave was treated as a piece of chattel by his owner. He could not speak unless spoken to, hold office or own property. He was on call at any hour day or night, and whether he lived or died depended entirely on the will of his master. That's why Paul's statement in Galatians 4:7 is so revolutionary. He says, "Therefore you are no longer a slave but a son." Sonship releases us from the bondage of being a slave into the freedom of being an intimate part of the family. As a son we have the freedom to:

Live by grace

The Law was necessary to bring men and women to the realization of God's absolute righteousness and their own sinfulness. Yet the Law was a cruel taskmaster. There was no flexibility in the Law: it was "do or die." Tragically, some Christians still want to live under similar restrictions because, for all its drawbacks, the Law was predictable and measurable. With a set of rules, you know exactly how to respond. There is no need to seek God's will; just refer to the list of rules. Plus, by living under the Law you always know where you stand. If you spend an hour in prayer, you get an A in God's grade book. If you pray only 15 minutes, however, something is obviously lacking and you need to rededicate yourself at the altar.

This is fine for a servant, but it's no way for a son to live. A servant has a master; a son has a father. The relationship between a master and slave is governed by rules; the relationship between a father and son should be governed by love. Where love dominates, the need for rules diminishes.

On the other hand, grace is not to be mistaken for license. Grace will never lead a son or daughter to violate God's moral standards. Grace will, however, lead you to live in a way that may run contrary to "common sense" as the world defines it. As I write, a couple of doctors in the family practice I use here in Lincoln, Nebraska, are preparing to leave their potentially lucrative practices and go overseas as career missionaries. The world says this is foolish. Grace says, "'Assuredly, I say to you, inasmuch as you did it to one of the least of these My brethren, you did it to Me'" (Matt. 25:40). Law doesn't understand grace, and neither do those who feel most comfortable living under the Law.

Grace living is a joyful abandonment to the will of God. A member of God's family doesn't live by "oughts"; he lives by "wants." Psalm 37:4 says, "Delight yourself also in the Lord, and He shall give you the desires of your heart." Lest this sound too radical, we need to remember that first comes the "delight yourself in the Lord," and then follows the "desires of your heart." But this is where grace comes in. Grace gives us that delight in the Lord, which makes His "will" our "want."

Anticipate the future

At one time Fiske Planetarium, on the campus of Colorado University, faced a serious financial need. In response, its director came up with what proved to be a profitable gimmick. He printed brochures that offered 1,000-acre lots on Mars for only $20. The flyer read: "This land still features pink skies, unlimited rock gardens, and not one but two moons. So peaceful, quiet, and romantic—even the natives are friendly." The literature also promised, "At one-sixth the gravity of Earth, your golf game will improve immensely—drives will be six times longer. Mars will provide a world of adventure for the entire family." In anticipation that perhaps someday space flight to Mars might be a reality, people across the country sent in $20 for a deed, for something called "space flight insurance" and for a simulated sample of red Martian soil. Needless to say, the planetarium was saved.

Such anticipation is a pale copy of what we Christians can look forward to—not as slaves, but as sons and daughters of our Heavenly Father. In the Roman world, slaves had little to anticipate. Since they could own no property, they built no equity. The best they could hope for was that their master might be kind enough to provide for them in their old age. This was far different from a son or daughter. They didn't need to fear the future because they knew that their father had much more than what was sufficient to meet their needs.

God's children need not fear the future either. In fact, not only do you have His promise to "supply all your needs according to His riches in glory by Christ Jesus" (Phil. 4:19), you have Jesus' unqualified promise, "I go to prepare a place for you. And if I go and prepare a place for you, I will come again and receive you to Myself; that where I am, there you may be also" (John 14:2–3). It is not surprising that Hudson Taylor could confidently say, "The future is as bright as the promises of God."

Live richly

Baron Mayer Rothschild, a member of the world-famous family of financiers, stepped from a carriage one evening and gave the driver what he felt was an adequate tip. Eyeing the tip disdainfully, the driver said, "Your lordship's son always gives me a good deal more than this."

"I daresay he does," Baron Rothschild snapped. "But then, you see, he has a rich father. I haven't."

The baron made an excellent point. When you have a father with plentiful resources to depend on, you don't have to worry about giving too much! In fact, it is a mark of confidence in the giver's wealth to give generously.

As sons and daughters of God, we have at our disposal all of His wealth, and God would have us give richly. Paul says, "So let each one give as he purposes in his heart, not grudgingly or of necessity; for God loves a cheerful giver. And God is able to make all grace abound toward you, that you, always having all sufficiency in all things, have an abundance for every good work" (2 Cor. 9:7-8). The Greek word for *cheerful* (*hilaros*) is the one from which we get our English word *hilarious*. It implies that we should surrender ourselves to the joy of giving. God, for His part, promises that we will have an "abundance for every good work."

Someone has said that there are three kinds of givers—the flint, the sponge and the honeycomb. If you try to get anything out of a flint, you have to hammer it. Even so, this tends only to produce sparks. If you want to get something from a sponge, you have squeeze it. It doesn't give of its own free will but waits for you to apply pressure. But the honeycomb overflows with its sweetness. It's this latter kind of giver that God wants us to be. We are to give generously, even hilariously, and trust Him for the resources. With sonship comes a freedom to live life richly, giving out of our abundance, knowing that our Father has plenty more to pass on.

The privilege of discipline

Thomas Jefferson wrote a friend, Mrs. Cosway, to offer this piece of advice: "The art of life is avoiding pain." The American culture has taken this advice and made it a maxim. Westerners are the most pain-conscious people in the world. One only has to stroll down the aisle of any drug store, supermarket or other retail outlet to notice that most carry an overwhelming number of pain remedies. It's not surprising, therefore, that many people think that only a masochist could possibly appreciate discipline and count it a privilege. Yet the writer of Hebrews reminds us, "My son, do not despise the chastening of the LORD, nor be discouraged when you are rebuked by Him" (12:5). Rather than being a cause for regret, God's discipline is an opportunity to rejoice. The writer goes on to give us several reasons why.

A sign of His love

Discipline means "to teach" (thus we have the word *disciples*, who are students of a teacher). True discipline is done in a spirit of love with the purpose of teaching the one being disciplined. That's why Proverbs 13:24 says, "He who spares his rod hates his son, but he who loves him disciplines him promptly." God deals with his sons and daughters this way because He loves them and wants the best for them.

Lou Holtz, football coach of the Fighting Irish of Notre Dame, declared, "When it comes to discipline here, we ask three questions: Will it make a better man? A better student? A better athlete? If the answer is yes, we make him do it."[2] In a sense, God has those same three principles in mind. The writer of Hebrews says, "For whom the LORD loves He chastens, and scourges every son whom He receives" (12:6). God treats us this way not because He is creating in us the image of a football player, but because He is creating in us the image of His Son.

Furthermore, God loves us so much He doesn't want to see us hurt ourselves. When you see your children doing things you know will harm them either now or later, it's only natural that you intercept them and teach them to do differently. Sometimes that means inflicting *some* pain now in order to prevent a *lot* of pain later. This takes a great deal of courage and self-denial on the part of a loving parent, because the one being disciplined will probably not appreciate it. Even the writer of Hebrews admits "no chastening seems to be joyful for the present, but grievous" (12:11). But when we love, we are willing to make the sacrifice.

God also knows how much we need discipline. The latter part of Hebrews 12:7 says, "for what son is there whom a father does not chasten?" In other words, what son is so perfect and knows how to do everything just right that he never needs to be taught through discipline? You can answer that for your own children, but the implied answer is, "None." Everyone needs to learn, and God loves us so much that He is not willing to allow any of us to hurt ourselves through ignorance. That's why He discipline us.

A sign of His ownership

When you see a child in the neighborhood doing something wrong, you may ask him to stop, but likely you won't discipline him unless he is your child. In fact, you might get in trouble with the law if you did. Basically, it's not our responsibility to raise our neighbors' children. It *is* our responsibility to raise our own, and that often involves disciplining them.

God operates on the same principle. "But if you are without chastening, of which all have become partakers, then you are illegitimate and not sons" (Heb. 12:8). It is not the person who is experiencing the discipline of the Lord who should be concerned—it's the person who isn't. God doesn't discipline the devil's children. He may allow hardship to come into their lives to show them how much they need Him, but He doesn't try to teach them to be holy or righteous. Until they come into a saving relationship with Jesus Christ, teaching holy living would be like trying to teach a blind man to see. It just won't happen.

A sign of hope

The most discouraging words in any language are *no hope.* These are the last words we want to hear from the doctor, the police or the rescuer. As terrible as it would be for someone to give up on us, think how much more terrible it would be for God to give up on us. You think that would never happen? He said to Noah, "My Spirit shall not strive with man forever" (Gen. 6:3). Paul says three times in Romans that God gave up. In 1:24 he says, "Therefore God also *gave them up* to uncleanness, in the lusts of their hearts, to dishonor their bodies among themselves" (italics mine). Verse 26 says, "For this reason God *gave them up* to vile passions. For even their women exchanged the natural use for what is against nature" (italics mine). And in verse 28 he says, "And even as they did not like to retain God in their knowledge, God *gave them over* to a debased mind, to do those things which are not fitting" (italics mine).

When God gives up it doesn't mean He doesn't have the power to save us. He always has that power. It means that there comes a time when God will no longer work to soften hearts toward Him and will simply allow sinners to reap the consequences of their sin. You don't have to look far today to see that happening in our society. Sometimes you even see God allowing Christians to reap the whirl-wind of unrepentant sin (Hos. 8:7). When God gives us up to the consequences of our sin, not much is left. On the other hand, as long as God continues to work with us through discipline to shape and form our character, we have hope. The writer of Hebrews promises us that God's discipline, even though painful, afterwards "yields the peaceable fruit of righteousness to those who have been trained by it" (12:11).

When we accept God's discipline, our lives become peaceable. We cease to have conflicts with God, demanding our own way, willfully pulling at the restraints that He has placed on us for our own good. The writer of Hebrews calls this "righteousness." In simplest terms, righteousness is a right (correct, proper) relationship with God. It is the relationship between a loving father and an obedient child. In this kind of relationship we have the hope—the sure expectation—that God will create in us the character of His Son.

An equal opportunity family

In some families certain children have more privileges than others. Because they are older, they may be allowed to stay up later or be gone more frequently with their friends. Because they are skilled, they may be privileged to spend more time in the game rather than warming the bench.

In God's family, however, we all have the same opportunity to access His privileges. We have become His sons and daughters through the saving grace of the Lord Jesus Christ. We have an equal opportunity to access the privileges of our position as the sons and daughters of a Heavenly Father. The privileges are there, but only you can take advantage of them for yourself. The rights are there, but only you can exercise them. The responsibilities are there, but only you can accept them. God has invited you into the joy of belonging to Him, but how much of that joy you experience depends, in large measure, on how you access His joy. Isn't it time you stepped up to the plate as a true son or daughter of the Heavenly Father?

---

1 "American Wealth!," *Brown Gold*, June 1980.

2 Gerry Kingdom, "Shaking Down the Thunder," *The Saturday Evening Post*, September 1989, p. 53.

Chapter 9

Belonging: The Promise of an Inheritance

As expected, Jacqueline Kennedy Onassis left the bulk of her estate to her two children, Caroline and John Jr. Her will, filed in New York, didn't disclose the full extent of her wealth (which has been estimated at up to $200 million), but it does provide a peek at the scope of her holdings. Caroline and John Jr. will inherit her 15-room Fifth Avenue apartment and its contents, plus other properties, including the Martha's Vineyard compound and $250,000 apiece. The will also establishes a charitable foundation, to be run by her two children, and grants them custody of her personal papers, which she asked to be kept private. In other bequests, stepbrother Hugh Auchincioss gets the cottage in Newport; longtime spokeswoman Nancy Tuckerman, whom Jackie described as "my close friend and confidante," inherits $250,000, and attorney Alexander Forger receives Jackie's personal copy of President John F. Kennedy's Inaugural speech, signed by poet Robert Frost. To companion Maurice Tempelsman she left her "Greek alabaster head of a woman." The children of her sister, Lee Radziwill Ross, also will receive income from a $1 million trust.[1]

To you and me, this is a magnificent inheritance, yet it doesn't begin to compare with the inheritance we have as part of God's family. When we receive Christ as our Savior, God the Father has reserved for us an inheritance that exceeds our comprehension. Scripture, however, does give us some idea of what this inheritance involves.

The focus of our inheritance

It's easy to limit our understanding of our inheritance from God to heavenly rewards. It is that—but also much more. An inheritance is to be enjoyed in the fullest measure possible. Our loving Father wants us to experience our inheritance the moment we discover the joy of belonging to Him. The focus of our inheritance, therefore, should include:

Our present inheritance

We usually think of an inheritance as something received after a person has died—but that's not necessarily true. For example, the Prodigal Son was acting foolishly when he demanded of his father, "'Give me the portion of goods that falls to me [i.e., my inheritance]'" (Luke 15:12); nevertheless, his request shows that it was possible for the son to receive an inheritance (or part of an inheritance) before his father passed away. That's our situation when we become a part of God's family. When we receive Christ, we immediately are given:

Salvation. Our salvation is both a present inheritance and a future one. Paul tells the Corinthians, "Behold, *now* is the accepted time; behold, *now* is the day of salvation" (2 Cor. 6:2, italics mine). In Titus 2:11 we read, "For the grace of God that brings salvation *has appeared* to all men" (italics mine). The Old Testament saints had to wait for their inheritance. In fact, many Bible scholars believe that Paradise was an area of Sheol, the place of the dead, where the faithful were kept. When Jesus told the story of Lazarus and the rich man (Luke 16:20-31), He indicated that the rich man could see Lazarus "in the bosom of Abraham" (i.e., Paradise) from his place in Hades, even though they were separated by an impassable gulf. Yet when Christ died on the cross, there was no more waiting. Ephesians 4:8 reveals that "when He ascended on high, He led captivity captive, and gave gifts to men." Some scholars understand this to be the occasion when those who had been held in Paradise were taken to heaven. While we cannot say that for certain, there is one thing we know for sure—on this side of the cross there is no waiting, but rather, "we are confident, yes, well pleased rather to be absent from the body and to be present with the Lord" (2 Cor. 5:8).

Salvation is a present reality for those who have trusted Jesus Christ as their Savior. As Paul says, "I am persuaded that neither death nor life, nor angels nor principalities nor powers, nor things present nor things to come, nor height nor depth, nor any other created thing, shall be able to separate us from the love of God which is in Christ Jesus our Lord" (Rom. 8:38-39). We are saved the moment we receive Jesus Christ as our personal Savior by faith. We are held securely in God's hands; nothing can separate us from Him, and no one can snatch us out of His hand (John 10:28–29). We must not be so futuristic in thinking of our inheritance that we lose sight of the fact that a glorious part of our salvation is here and now.

Yet there is an equally glorious aspect to our salvation still to come, when "the Lord comes with ten thousands of His saints" (Jude 1:14) and those who are living shall be bodily transformed and caught up in the air, "and thus we shall always be with the Lord" (1 Thess. 4:17).

Today we have our salvation in part, but not in total. Our souls are saved and as safe as if we had already been in heaven a million years. But our physical being, including all the rest of physical creation, is still waiting for ultimate salvation. Paul says, "For we know that the whole creation groans and labors with birth pangs together until now. And not only they, but we also who have the firstfruits of the Spirit, even we ourselves groan within ourselves, eagerly waiting for the adoption, the redemption of our body (Rom. 8:22–23). This redemption will come only when Christ returns for His Church. At that point "the Lord Himself will descend from heaven with a shout, with the voice of an archangel, and with the trumpet of God. And the dead in Christ will rise first" (1 Thess. 4:16). This resurrection does not refer to our souls, because they are already with Christ. Rather, it refers to the raising of our physical bodies, "for the trumpet will sound, and the dead will be raised incorruptible, and we shall be changed. For this corruptible must put on incorruption, and this mortal must put on immortality" (1 Cor. 15:52-53).

Promises. Not only do we confidently possess salvation as part of our inheritance, we also have confidence in all the promises of God. In exhorting his readers to faithfulness, the writer of Hebrew says, "And we desire that each one of you show the same diligence to the full assurance of hope until the end, that you do not become sluggish, but imitate those who through faith and patience *inherit the promises*" (6:11-12, italics mine).

It is estimated that there are 7,487 promises in the Bible. Not all of them, of course, directly relate to Christians or the New Testament Church. Some relate to God's chosen people, Israel, and the family of Abraham (for example, see Genesis 17:1-8; 26:1-5; 28:1-4). Others concern the role of Israel during the Millennium (the thousand-year reign of Christ on earth), such as Zephaniah 3:13 and Zechariah 14:16-21. Still others of God's promises have been fulfilled and we no longer wait for them (for example, those dealing with the first coming of Christ). Yet even with those removed, that leaves thousands of promises for us to claim and inculcate into our lives. There is the promise of incomprehensible peace (Phil. 4:7), the pledge that God is able and willing to meet all our needs (4:19), the assurance of Christ's presence with us always (Matt. 28:20)—and these are only a few. In his devotional *Faith's Checkbook,* Charles Spurgeon suggests a list of promises that can be claimed for each day of the year — and that doesn't even come close to exhausting all the promises of God. There are enough of His promises recorded in the Bible to keep us exhilarated forever, if only we believe and claim them.

I make it a habit to underline the verses in my Bible where God makes a promise to His children. It has always been a tremendous encouragement to my family and me. Someone has correctly observed that "God is the God of promises. He keeps His word, even when that seems impossible, even when the circumstances seem to point to the opposite." Numbers 23:19 inquires, "God is not a man, that He should lie, . . . Has He said, and will He not do? Or has He spoken, and will He not make it good?" After D. L. Moody died, his family looked through his Bible and found on almost every page, in the margins, the letters "T" and "P." "T" indicated he had tried the promise, and the "P" indicated that he had proved a promise to be true in his life. Moody's experience can be yours, if you are willing to claim your inheritance.

Our future inheritance

Grand as our salvation and God's promises are, the Bible indicates that there is more to our inheritance than meets the eye, at least than that has met our eyes so far. In Romans 8:17 Paul says that once we have discovered the joy of belonging, we are "heirs of God and joint heirs with Christ, if indeed we suffer with Him, that we may also be glorified together." The phrase "joint heirs" is translated in some versions as "coheirs." A coheir is one who has the same inheritance as all the other heirs. Think of it! You and I are destined to inherit everything that Christ inherits. Perhaps this makes little impression on you. It's hard to comprehend, I admit. But think of what the Bible says Christ will inherit. Hebrews 1:1-2 reveals, "God, who at various times and in different ways spoke in time past to the fathers by the prophets, has in these last days spoken to us by His Son, *whom He has appointed heir of all things*" (italics mine).

We can no more comprehend "all things" than we can grasp the concept of eternity. These things escape our minds because they go beyond our limited human understanding. But you have to agree that "all things" surely points toward a future of unlimited potential. And that future is yours, if you know Christ Jesus as your Savior and Lord. It's all part of your inheritance in Christ. The wealth of the richest man or nation can't compare with that!

The conditions of our inheritance

A drawback of human wills is that not everyone is a beneficiary. In the case of Jacqueline Kennedy Onassis, there were certain conditions that had to be met before someone was named as one of her heirs. One of the more important conditions was having a close relationship with her, such as friend or relative, and even that did not guarantee inclusion. God also places some conditions on those who would benefit from His will. If we want to claim an inheritance, we must be:

Righteous

As mentioned in the last chapter, righteousness has to do with a right relationship with God. There are two ways we can try to have a relationship with God: through our own efforts or by accepting the payment Christ made on our behalf at the cross. Whichever we choose, there are two conditions we must meet.

First, we must be completely holy and entirely pure, because that is the character of God. He will not share His inheritance with anyone who is unworthy of Him. As 2 Corinthians 6:14 says, "Do not be unequally yoked together with unbelievers. For what fellowship has righteousness with lawlessness? And what communion has light with darkness?" This command is directed toward Christians, but what's true for us is also true for God. How can God have fellowship with those who are stained with sin? Even if He wanted to, God could not allow His purity to coexist with sin any more than a lighted match could continue to burn inside an ice cube. These things are mutually exclusive; one would destroy the other.

Second, we must deal with our past sins. Romans 3:23 declares, "For all have sinned and fall short of the glory of God." Let's consider a hypothetical example. Suppose you found a way from this day on to live a holy, perfect life. Never again would you sin in thought, word or deed. Sounds wonderful, doesn't it? But as fantastic as that would be, you still have a significant problem: what to do with your past sins. Until you do something about those sins, they will haunt you even if you lived a holy and pure life from this point on.

It's just like having past bills. Suppose you spent a great deal more than you could afford buying Christmas presents for your friends and family. Since you don't have the cash to pay for them, you charge them to your credit card. Now Christmas is over and you would like to forget about those bills, but you can't. Every month you get a reminder of your extravagance from the credit card company. The company wants to be paid. You can't ignore your debt or pretend it doesn't exist. It won't go away by itself. The only solution is to pay your credit card, but what if you can't? What do you do then?

Similarly, on our own we can't achieve the righteousness of God. Our human nature is rotten to the core, and, unless something is drastically changed, we can never be righteous enough to enjoy a relationship with God. Paul says,

> Now the works of the flesh are evident, which are: adultery, fornication, uncleanness, licentiousness, idolatry, sorcery, hatred, contentions, jealousies, outbursts of wrath, selfish ambitions, dissensions, heresies, envy, murders, drunkenness, revelries, and the like; of which I tell you beforehand, just as I also told you in time past, that those who practice such things will not inherit the kingdom of God (Gal. 5:19).

This fleshly character, as Paul describes it in Galatians, is incompatible with God's character. The two can't coexist. That's why God can't simply improve our character; He must replace it. When we receive Christ as our Savior, our character is changed to reflect Christ's character, which is holy and pure.

Even so, we still have to deal with our past sins. How can they be paid for? Should we sin again (which is inevitable), how will those sins be dealt with? The answer is the same for both of these questions. Only the blood of Jesus Christ can cleanse us from sin—past, present and future. The writer of Hebrews says, "For if the blood of bulls and goats and the ashes of a heifer, sprinkling the unclean, sanctifies for the purifying of the flesh, how much more shall the blood of Christ, who through the eternal Spirit offered Himself without spot to God, purge your conscience from dead works to serve the living God?" (9:13–14).

Sin requires that a life be given. Romans 6:23 says, "For the wages of sin is death." In the Old Testament the blood of bulls and goats was used as a token of this death. God says in Leviticus 17:11, "For the life of the flesh is in the blood, and I have given it to you upon the altar to make atonement for your souls; for it is the blood that makes atonement for the soul." But this was only symbolic of the greater sacrifice that would be made by One called the "Lamb of God"—Jesus Christ.

Paul declares, "In Him we have redemption *through His blood*, the forgiveness of sins, according to the riches of His grace" (Eph. 1:7, italics mine). Again in Ephesians 2:13, "But now in Christ Jesus you who once were far off *have been made near by the blood of Christ*" (italics mine). When King David sinned, he cried to God, "Restore to me the joy of Your salvation" (Ps. 51:12). Sin separates us from God and the joy of belonging, but the blood of Christ cleanses us from sin, brings us near to God and restores that joy.

Faithful

Faithfulness is another condition for receiving our inheritance. Hebrews 11:6 states, "Without faith it is impossible to please Him, for he who comes to God must believe that He is, and that He is a rewarder of those who diligently seek Him." Yet how do we show our faith? By being faithful.

Abraham trusted God. He believed God was working out the very best for him and his family. Therefore,

> By faith Abraham obeyed when he was called to go out to the place which he would afterward receive as an inheritance. And he went out, not knowing where he was going. By faith he sojourned in the land of promise as in a foreign country, dwelling in tents with Isaac and Jacob, the heirs with him of the same promise; for he waited for the city which has foundations, whose builder and maker is God (Heb. 11:8-10).

Abraham demonstrated his faith by his faithfulness in obeying God.

God's inheritance is not for those who say they have faith, but for those who show it through their faithfulness. There is a legend of a wealthy woman who, when she reached heaven, was shown a very plain mansion. She objected. "Well," the angel said, "that is the house prepared for you."

"Whose is that fine mansion across the way?" she asked.

"It belongs to your gardener," the angel replied.

"How is it that he has one so much better than mine?"

"The houses here are prepared from the materials that are sent up. We do not choose them. You do that by your earthly faithfulness."

The Christian race is not a competitive event to see who comes in first, but an endurance run to see who finishes faithfully. Jesus encourages us to look forward to that day when God shall say, "Well done, good and faithful servant; you were faithful over a few things, I will make you ruler over many things. Enter into the joy of your lord" (Matt. 25:21, 23).

Patient

Patience is seldom considered a standard for our inheritance, but only because we are so poor at it. The writer of Hebrews exhorts his readers, "We desire that each one of you show the same diligence to the full assurance of hope until the end, that you do not become sluggish, but imitate those who through faith and *patience* inherit the promises" (6:11-12, italics mine).

If we want to inherit all that God has for us, we must wait patiently. We may be like Fred Roberts from Alamitos, California. Mr. Roberts was a corporal in Company D, 151st Machine Gun Battalion, 42nd Rainbow Division in World War I. As his company was advancing from Champagne Feront into the Belleau Woods during the second Battle of the Marne in France, they were caught in an artillery barrage that included mustard gas. Roberts was treated for gas inhalation and shell shock. That was in 1918. In return for his valor, Mr. Roberts was awarded a Purple Heart—in March 1995 at the age of 99. His comment? "They must have lost my records." [2]

God, however, never forgets and never loses a record. Those who are faithful will find Him totally faithful. Even though it is delayed, our inheritance is coming.

Furthermore, we also need to exercise our patience so we will not give in. Even if we don't give up, we might be enticed to give in and accept a solution other than God's. This is where Abraham faltered. Though God had told him explicitly he would have a son by his wife, Sarah, as the years passed by and he didn't see an answer to that promise, Abraham gave in and took Hagar as his concubine. He got his son (Ishmael), but he got a great deal of grief and heartache as well. The world is always ready to offer you an alternative to God's plan, but it never works out for your best. Be patient. Don't give up on God and never give in.

The assurance of our inheritance

I saw a bumper sticker on a recreational vehicle that read, "We're spending our children's inheritance." While I'm sure that was meant as a joke, if it were true, this couple's children are in for a big surprise. Imagine them gathering for the reading of the will only to find out that nothing was left for them. Could that happen to God's sons and daughters? The Bible says no and give us three assurances that we will receive an inheritance.

The Father planned our inheritance

Colossians 1:12 says, "Giving thanks to the Father who has qualified us to be partakers of the inheritance of the saints in the light." The word translated "qualified" is *hikanoo*, which means "to make able." When God the Father drew up the plan of salvation, which includes our inheritance, He also included in those plans a way for us to meet the standards that we might "qualify" to receive our inheritance. John hints of this when he describes Jesus as "the Lamb slain from the foundation of the world" (Rev. 13:8). From the very beginning God had intended to help us qualify for our inheritance by giving His Son as the only acceptable sacrifice for our sins. Since God was willing to plan for that kind of sacrifice, surely He must have a marvelous inheritance waiting for us.

The Son provided our inheritance

The Father drew up the plan, but it took the Son's cooperation for the plan to take effect. Christ had to be willing to die on the cross.

The cross had no hidden secrets from Christ. When He came to earth to be born and live among men, He knew what kind of hideous death He would suffer. He knew the crucifixion would be a shameful atrocity. It was the form of death reserved for the most despised criminals. The bodies of those who died on the cross usually were not even buried; they were thrown onto the town's garbage heap.

Jesus knew His would be a physically agonizing death. He first would be scourged with whips—leather thongs with pieces of bone or metal at the ends. Then He would be laid on the cross, nails driven through each hand and foot. Then the cross would be lifted upright and dropped into a hole in the ground, ripping His flesh. His death would not come quickly. It would be painful and slow. But Jesus knew it would be a spiritually agonizing death as well. Never in all of eternity had the Triune Godhead been separated from one another. But as Jesus suffered on the cross, He would cry out in spiritual agony, "My God, My God, why have You forsaken Me?" (Matt. 27:46). Jesus endured the suffering and shame of crucifixion so that "in Him" we can have an inheritance. He is our assurance.

The Holy Spirit protects our inheritance

In 1993 Sotheby's auction in New York City offered for sale a seal used to stamp official documents with the imprint of the owner. The 1" x 2/3" piece of orange chalcedony rock bore the name of a high official in the courts of Hoshea, the last king of Israel, before it was overrun by the Assyrians. The inscription read, "Belonging to Abdi servant of Hoshea." When the hammer fell on December 14, 1993, the seal fetched $80,000.

Those who have received Christ have a far more valuable seal that stamps them as "official." Paul writes in Ephesians 1:13-14, "In Him you also trusted, after you heard the word of truth, the gospel of your salvation; in whom also, having believed, *you were sealed with the Holy Spirit of promise, who is the guarantee of our inheritance* until the redemption of the purchased possession, to the praise of His glory" (italics mine). Our inheritance is not only planned by the Father and purchased by the Son, it is also protected by seal of the Holy Spirit. No one can say, "But this inheritance cannot be for you. Look at what you have been." It's at that point that God will remind us not of what we have been, but of who we are in Christ Jesus. We are heirs of God and joint-heirs with Christ. God's seal confirms that we are His legitimate heirs.

Count your blessings

There are times when we may envy those whose rich relatives leave them valuable treasures in their wills. Yet we must never forget that we, too, have an inheritance. It is not only more fantastic than any recorded here on earth, it is also imperishable. It will never fade, melt, rust or slip away. It is ours forever, and we are already beginning to see the benefits of being a part of the family of God. Our inheritance is already in place, and we are partially enjoying it right now. But there is much more to come.

This is not the time to salivate over the earthly good fortunes of others. It's the time to count your blessings. Estates can be devalued and deteriorate. Money can slip through your fingers like water. But as a child of the King, you have an inheritance that is reserved in your name and kept by God's power (1 Pet. 1:4–5). This is a time to rejoice, count your blessings and rediscover the joy of belonging to God as an heir.

---

[1] "Jackie O.'s Other Legacy," *Newsweek*, June 13, 1994, p. 50.

[2] "Purple Heart recipient is a very patient man," *Indianapolis Star*, March 14, 1995, p. D-2.

Chapter 10

Belonging: The Company of the Committed

When we become a member of God's family, we immediately acquire brothers and sisters all over the world. God's family includes all those people who, like we, have been regenerated and baptized with the Holy Spirit into the body of Christ. We call that body the Church (with a capital "C"). It includes those, both living and dead, who are "in Christ"—that is, who are born again by the grace of God. This universal body is sometimes called the "Invisible Church" because it can't be see in its totality. The family members we have most contact with, however, are the body of believers we call the local church (with a lowercase "c"). These are the people who gather regularly from a particular geographical area for the purpose of worship and ministry. We may meet under a variety of names, but we have at least one thing in common: we are born again, banded together to do the work of God in this world.

When we become a part of the Church, we should prayerfully ask God to lead us to the right church for us. It should be a church that demonstrates a desire to glorify God, to reach unsaved people in its community with the redeeming message of the Gospel and to take that message to the ends of the earth through an aggressive missions program. The right church for you will draw its doctrine directly out of the Bible. It should be a place where you can be spiritually fed from challenging messages preached from Scripture by an anointed servant of the Word. Also important is that it be a church where you can use your spiritual gifts in service to the Lord. If all these needs are met, it's a strong indication that this is the church God has for you.

Churches have changed in many ways over the last few decades. If you haven't grown up in the church or haven't been active in the church, you might be in for some culture shock. To minimize this, we need to keep in mind that:

God's people are special

We all have special people in our lives. Maybe it's your spouse or a favorite aunt or uncle. It could even be a best friend. These people are special because they meet a need in our lives that no one else can. In the same way, God's people are special.

Christians share the same concern for God's glory

We can join many groups who share a common concern. There are groups concerned about recycling, saving the whales, protecting the ozone layer, etc. People in the church may be concerned about these things as well, but predominantly they are concerned about God's glory. The primary purpose of the church is to reveal God's glory to the world. The church accomplishes this by sharing the message of God's love and grace, which culminated in sending His Son to die on the cross for our sins. Christians also demonstrate the righteousness and holiness of God's character through the way they live and respond to situations around them.

I have nothing against these other groups. I try to recycle, I love watching whales, and I'm concerned about the ozone layer, especially when I'm out in my lawn with the sun beating down on my head. But at the bottom line, these are only temporal concerns. All the trash (and everything else) will some day burn up (2 Pet. 3:7), whales will cease to exist (Revelation 21:1 says "there was no more sea"), and even the ozone layer will become an irrelevant issue (2 Pet. 3:10). While it is right to be concerned about these things, we must remember that the only eternal issue we face today is the glory of God. There is only one group that will share this concern with you, and that is the people of God.

Christians intercede for you with God

God has given His people the great privilege of praying for each other. Lidia Vins, mother of Georgi Vins,[1] a Russian Christian sentenced twice to a Siberian labor camp for his belief in the Gospel, wrote concerning her son: "When I saw him during the trial, tormented and pale, with sunken eyes, I thought, *He hasn't slept for nights*. The trial lasted five days. But when we parted he said, 'I was able to go to sleep peacefully every night. It was a very great mercy of God. It is surely due to the many prayers of God's children.'"

Lidia Vins said that she had the same experience in prison, and so have many others. "Many who have been in prison have testified that they felt people's prayers, and they knew not simply those days when they were prayed for, but the actual hours. This is the testimony of more than one prisoner," she wrote.

The prayers of His people move the hand of God. As someone commented in referring to Peter's imprisonment in Acts 12, "The angel fetched Peter out of prison, but it was prayer that fetched the angel." No other group can claim this kind of power. It is a privilege that God has reserved only for His Church, and you can reap the benefit when you belong.

Christians discourage sin

Jim, a friend of mine who is a recovering alcoholic, was employed in the construction trade. Often he was ignored on the job because he wouldn't go to the tavern after work with the other guys. These men knew Jim's weakness, but they still tried to pressure him into taking a drink.

This reminds me again how often people encourage us to do wrong and how seldom they persuade us to do right. In 1991 a convention of the Tailhook Association was held at the Las Vegas Hilton. During that time as many as 200 Navy and Marine flyers formed a "poke-and-grab gauntlet along a third-floor corridor." Eighty-three women claim they were assaulted. Not one person, including some of the higher-level officers who were there, protested the behavior.[2]

What a contrast this is to Christian gatherings. I have been to many conventions where thousands of believers have come together without a single episode of drunkenness, lewd conduct or disorderliness. Why is this? It's due, in part, to the presence of the Holy Spirit. Paul says, "The mystery of lawlessness is already at work; only He who now restrains will do so until He is taken out of the way" (2 Thess. 2:7). Many people understand this "restrainer" to be the Holy Spirit. When we have the Holy Spirit in our lives, He makes us sensitive to sin and convicts us of sin when we fail to obey.

But the presence of other Christians is also a restraining influence. No Christian wants to see a brother or sister fall into sin. In fact James says, "Brethren, if anyone among you wanders from the truth, and someone turns him back, let him know that he who turns a sinner from the error of his way will save a soul from death and cover a multitude of sins" (James 5:19–20). A Christian is responsible, in as far as he is able, to help another believer avoid sin. It is wrong for him to cause his brother to stumble, even indirectly (1 Cor. 8:12–13). This reinforcement to live righteously makes belonging to a local body of believers such a joy.

God's people are imperfect

Unfortunately, another side to the church also exists. New Christians are sometimes quite shocked when they come face-to-face with some of the glaring flaws of God's people. As one person put it, "The church is like Noah's ark. If it weren't for the storm on the outside, you couldn't stand the stink on the inside." Thankfully, it's not always that way, but sometimes it is. Why? There are three fundamental reasons:

Christians are humans

When Adam and Eve disobeyed, our human natures were significantly bent out of shape. Genesis 3 records the events of the Fall and the seeds of conflict. When God confronted Adam about his sin, he responded, "The woman whom You gave to be with me, she gave me of the tree, and I ate" (v. 12). Every married person knows that one of the ways to start a fight is to blame your spouse for something you've done instead of taking responsibility for it yourself.

In Genesis 4 that blaming led to something worse than a quarrel. When God rejected Cain's offering but accepted Abel's, Cain blamed Abel and becomes so angry that he killed him (v. 8). Without question, the consequences of blaming are bitter, yet we still play that game both in our families and in the church.

We forget that when a person receives Christ and his old nature is crucified, he still has habits and influences solidly ingrained from the practices of past years. Some of these habits are as stubborn as crab grass. It takes the work of God's Spirit, as well as personal effort, to eradicate them.

In the meantime, we should consider our own lives. Whenever someone would come to D. L. Moody with a bad report about somebody else, he would reply, "Right now

I'm having so much trouble with D. L. Moody that I don't have time to find fault with the other fellow." When we are aware of our own sins, we can be more gracious in dealing with the sins of others.

Don't let conflict surprise you. Until the Lord comes again, there will be pockets of conflict in the church. After all, we are still sinners, even if we are saved. As the bumper sticker says, "I'm not perfect, just saved."

Christians are in spiritual warfare

Human nature, however, is only part of the reason for conflict in the church. Another important cause is that we are engaged in spiritual warfare. Paul says, "For we do not wrestle against flesh and blood, but against principalities, against powers, against the rulers of the darkness of this age, against spiritual hosts of wickedness in the heavenly places" (Eph. 6:12).

Part of Satan's battle plan is to render the Church as ineffective as possible. This is not true for any other group. Satan couldn't care less if people meet for social reasons, for physical fitness or to rally around some cause. None of this intimidates him. But God's people threaten him (unless they are meeting for social reasons, physical fitness or some other cause). The Church can restrain Satan's evil deeds and will some day participate in his destruction (1 Cor. 6:3).

Consequently, Satan takes every opportunity to stir up trouble. You may have heard of the ubiquitous Tate family. There is Dick Tate, who wants to run everything. Ro Tate tries to change everything. Agi Tate just likes to stir up trouble whenever possible (and Irri Tate always lends him a hand). Whenever new ideas are suggested, Hesi Tate and Vegi Tate pour cold water on them. Imi Tate tries to mimic everyone, Devas Tate loves to be disruptive, and Poten Tate wants to be a big shot. Sadly, every church has it share of the Tates, and Satan is an expert at manipulating them.

It doesn't help that, for the most part, churches are ignorant of the fact that they are in a spiritual battle. When trouble crops up, they try to deal with surface issues and neglect the deeper spiritual causes. They turn to the methods used by secular groups, which have no power against spiritual forces. As a result churches are failing at an alarming rate. George Barna, founder and president of the Barna Research Group, observes, "Almost every measure of religious behavior we have available is currently at, or near, its low point for the past decade. This includes church attendance, Bible reading, adult Sunday School attendance and small-group participation."[3]

"Christians" aren't always Christians

The word *Christian* has a number of meanings in our society. When someone says, "I'm a Christian," he may simply mean he is not a Buddhist, Hindu or animist. He may not even know what a Christian is.

For others, the word is more of a political stance than a way of life. This is true, for example, in Germany, which has the Christian Democrat Party. In the beginning this group may have had ties with the Christian faith, but such connections no longer exist.

In the same fashion, there are those in the church who go by the name "Christian" but have not experienced the new birth. Only God, of course, truly knows a person's heart, but Jesus warned, "Beware of false prophets, who come to you in sheep's clothing, but inwardly they are ravenous wolves" (Matt. 7:15). Works that we generally associate with the Christian faith, such as giving, witnessing and even seemingly supernatural manifestations, are not indisputable proofs of the joy of belonging. Jesus said, "Many will say to Me in that day, 'Lord, Lord, have we not prophesied in Your name, cast out demons in Your name, and done many wonders in Your name?' And then I will declare to them, 'I never knew you; depart from Me, you who practice lawlessness!'" (vv. 22–23).

While it is God's responsibility to judge, it is our responsibility to discern. When difficulties arise in the church, is the cause immaturity, carnality or unbelief? The root problem will determine how we respond to the situation.

Christians are necessary

Sometimes when we encounter people and situations in the church that hurt us, we're tempted to throw in the towel and quit. That has happened more than once with tragic results. Mark Twain became bitter at the church because of the discrepancies he saw in what was preached and what was practiced. Consequently, he refused to have anything to do with organized religion. Yet this didn't make him happy. By the time he died, the man who had been known as a humorist was better known as a cynic.

God never intended for us to be Lone Ranger Christians. Unless there are extraordinary circumstances for which He gives us special grace, God's plan is for us to be a part of a local group of believers. In fact, the writer of Hebrews commands us, "Let us consider one another in order to stir up love and good works, *not forsaking the assembling of ourselves together*, as is the manner of some, but exhorting one another, and so much the more as you see the Day approaching" (Heb. 10:24-25, italics mine). Meeting together as a body of believers is necessary because it is a:

Source of fellowship

The English word *fellowship* comes from the Anglo-Saxon word *fee-lowship*. A fee was a cow, and cows represented wealth (hence we get our word *fee*, which means a payment of money). When people really trusted each other, they broke down the walls and fences between their fields and allowed their cows to graze together. You might say they established a joint bank account.[4] Their "fee-lowship" was more than having pie and coffee together; it was a matter of sharing their lives together in the bonds of mutual trust.

This is the essence of what Christian fellowship is. It begins in a trusting relationship with God. Jesus said, "He who has My commandments and keeps them, it is he who loves Me. And he who loves Me will be loved by My Father, and I will love him and manifest Myself to him. . . . If anyone loves Me, he will keep My word; and My Father will love him, and We will come to him and make Our home with him" (John 14:21, 23). From this vertical fellowship comes our fellowship with others. In the Book of Acts, Luke records what fellowship was like in the early church.

> And they continued steadfastly in the apostles' doctrine and fellowship, in the breaking of bread, and in prayers. . . . Now all who believed were together, and had all things in common, and sold their possessions and goods, and divided them among all, as anyone had need. So continuing daily with one accord in the temple, and breaking bread from house to house, they ate their food with gladness and simplicity of heart, praising God and having favor with all the people (2:42-47).

When we look at these verses we find several characteristics that should be a part of our fellowship as well. When it is pleasing to God, fellowship is:

Focused on God. When these people met together, their topic of conversation was the "apostles' doctrine." That which distinguishes Christian fellowship from all other types of the fellowship is the focus of our conversation. We may chat about the weather or discuss some recent sporting event, but unless Christians go deeper than these superficial subjects, we aren't having real fellowship. It's also true that when we allow our focus to stray from God and His

Word, we are more likely to end up with a gossip session than a fellowship time.

Expressed in generosity. Fellowship has to be expressed in more than words. The apostle John says, "My little children, let us not love in word or in tongue, but in deed and in truth" (1 John 3:18). The early Christians made significant sacrifices for each other. We are fellowshipping to a much greater degree and for a much more satisfying reason when we join together to rake a widow's yard than when we gather for a "fellowship" dinner. Fellowship should be generous and purposeful.

Resulting in praise. Ultimately, fellowship is for God's glory, not just our pleasure. Fellowship is proof that the love of God can overcome any social, economic or racial barrier. Luke says that those in the church "praised God" and those outside the church expressed "favor." William Barclay translates it, "and everyone liked them."[5] A church that knows how to truly fellowship is a cause of praise to God for everyone.

Source of spiritual growth

When most people think of a biblical scholar, they envision a man locked in an ivory tower pouring over old manuscripts. There may be some truth to that. Scholarship requires a great deal of time spent in study. God, however, doesn't call too many of us to be scholars, but He calls all of us to be students. Paul says, "And this I pray, that your love may abound still more and more in knowledge and all discernment, that you may approve the things that are excellent, that you may be sincere and without offense till the day of Christ" (Phil. 1:9–10). This is not the knowledge that "puffs up" in pride (1 Cor. 8:1); it's the knowledge that draws us closer to God.

Where do we get such knowledge? One important source is the church. As we gather to participate in worship, in Sunday school and in Bible studies, God uses other Christians in the power of His Holy Spirit to bring us to a greater understanding and application of His Word. Proverbs says, "As iron sharpens iron, so a man sharpens the countenance of his friend" (27:17). We won't find spiritual knowledge at Rotary, the Lions or the health club; we'll find it only in God's special place—the church.

A place to belong

Each spring my wife, Linda, plants a flower garden. She loves doing it and is quite creative in her efforts. Rather than plant a row of flowers, she plants a "clump." The flowers are grouped together in clusters of diverse color. What looks thin and unimpressive planted in a row looks plush and beautiful together. Christians are like that too. We need others for all the reasons listed above and many more.

In his book *Great Church Fights*, Leslie Flynn tells of two porcupines in the cold north country. Because of the extreme cold, the porcupines huddled together for warmth. But when they did, their quills jabbed and pricked each other. Flynn likened these porcupines to Christians when he observed, "They needed each other, even though they needled each other."

If you belong to God's family universal, you need to belong to God's family locally. It's not a perfect family, but it's better than anything the world has to offer. It's the privilege of the believer—part of the joy of belonging.

---

[1] Georgi Vins was born in 1928. His fater, Peter, was arrested three times for preaching the Gospel. He died in a Siberian labor camp in 1943 when Georgi was only seven years old. In 1966 Georgi was arrested for the same "crime" as his father—preaching the Gospel—and spent three years in prison. In 1974 he was arrested again and sentenced to ten years in a labor camp. Halfway through he was released, stripped of his Soviet citizenship and exiled to the United States. His family was allowed to join him six weeks later. He credits his protection and deliverance to the power of God and the prayers of Christian believers.

[2] Richard Lacayo, "Lost in the Fun House," *Time*, February 21, 1994, p. 45.

[3] George Barna, *Virtual America* (Ventura, Calif.: Regal Books, 1994), p. 45.

[4] Ray Ortlund, *Lord, Make My Life a Miracle* (Ventura, Calif.: Gospel Light, 1974), p. 64.

[5] William Barclay, *The Acts of the Apostles* (Philadelphia: The Westmnister Press, 1976), p. 29.

Chapter 11

Belonging: Responding to New Leadership

Nineteen ninety-five was a year of significant adjustments for the Big Eight Conference. Half of the football teams in the conference had new head coaches—Iowa State, Oklahoma State, Oklahoma and Colorado. You can imagine all the changes that took place as each coach implemented his philosophy for winning football games.

When you join the family of God, you also come under the influence of a new head Coach. You can expect some significant changes. Life will never be the same. You are operating out of a new playbook. You have a new teacher, a new influence, a new everything. As 2 Corinthians 5:17 points out, "If anyone is in Christ, he is a new creation; old things have passed away; behold, all things have become new." But what if the old coach won't disappear? What if he won't leave without a fight? You're excited about the presence of the new Coach, but what about the old coach?

The old coach

The apostle Paul tells his friend Titus, "Remind them to be subject to rulers and authorities, to obey, to be ready for every good work, to speak evil of no one, to be peaceable, gentle, showing all humility to all men. For we ourselves were also once foolish, disobedient, deceived, serving various lusts and pleasures, living in malice and envy, hateful and hating one another" (Titus 3:1-3). According to Paul, that's the way we *were*—past tense. That's how the old coach, Satan, ran his team. That's the way he taught all his players to play the game of life. It's not a pretty picture. If a person could step back and objectively view the plays in Satan's playbook, who could blame him for quitting? Unfortunately, most people prefer to stay on his team. Paul describes those who chose to be on Satan's team as ones "whose minds the god of this age has blinded, who do not believe, lest the light of the gospel of the glory of Christ, who is the image of God, should shine on them" (2 Cor. 4:4).

A picture that hangs in a gallery in London is one of the most tragic pictures ever painted. It portrays the rough slope of a mountain that leads to the edge of a precipice, at the foot of which is a misty graveyard. A crowd of men and women pack the slope—some in evening dress, some in work clothes, some in rags—all struggling for a foothold and treading on one another. They are staring upward, where the beckoning, mocking figure of pleasure floats out of their reach. The picture is called "The Pursuit of Pleasure." On that grim, ghostly canvas the artist painted not one happy face; not a smile, not a flicker of gladness; nothing but fear, hatred, selfishness and pain.

Many people can identify with the hopelessness of this painting. One California psychiatrist noted that four out of every ten teenagers who visit his medical center have a psychological sickness he can do nothing about. According to the *Los Angeles Times,* "Each of them demands that his world conform to his uncontrolled desires. Society has provided him with so many escape routes that he never has to stand his ground against disappointment, postponement of pleasure and the weight of responsibility—all forces which shape character." The psychiatrist adds, "If the personality disorder persists far into adulthood, there will be a society of pleasure-driven people hopelessly insecure and dependent."

Frankly, with players like that on the team, there isn't much hope for a winning season. The only sensible thing to do is to quit the team and find yourself a new head coach. That's exactly what happened when we became a member of God's family. We quit the old team and joined a new one. We told the old coach to hit the road. We now receive our plays from a new head Coach, but that means we have to play by a new game plan. We can't live the way we did under the old coach. The rules have changed. The old strategies in Satan's playbook are no longer appropriate for us. Paul says, "When the kindness and the love of God our Savior toward man appeared, not by works of righteousness which we have done, but according to His mercy He saved us, through the washing of regeneration and renewing of the Holy Spirit" (Titus 3:4-5). When a new coach comes to town, we have to make sure the old coach knows we are no longer interested in playing for him. We have a much better option.

The new Coach

It's a big challenge to adjust to new leadership. It means we can't put our plane on automatic pilot and let it fly by itself anymore. We have to think before we act. We have to pull ourselves out of the old ruts and learn new ways to play the game. When we receive Christ, the Holy Spirit comes to be our coach. Jesus said, "And I will pray the Father, and He will give you another Helper, that He may abide with you forever; the Spirit of truth, whom the world cannot receive, because it neither sees Him nor knows Him; but you know Him, for He dwells with you and will be in you" (John 14:16–17). Later Jesus again said, "But the Helper, the Holy Spirit, whom the Father will send in My name, He will teach you all things, and bring to your remembrance all things that I said to you" (v. 26).

When the old coach is rejected, God doesn't leave us without a coach. Instead He provides One who dwells within us. Imagine having your mentor with you at all times. You would have to be foolish to try to run the old plays with the new Coach inside of you. Does the presence of the new head Coach mean you will never lose yardage? Not at all. You'll run face-first into some pretty tough blocking, but the outcome of the game will never again be in doubt. It won't be easy playing for the new Coach; old habits are hard to break. Still, it can be done if you are willing to implement the following suggestions.

Welcome the Coach

When we compare how different our lives are under the ministry of our new Coach, it should become evident what a good deal we are getting. Instead of a cruel taskmaster, He is our helper. Instead of leading us into tangled webs of deception, He teaches us the truth. Instead of playing for ourselves, He teaches us how to play for the team. What a pleasing change the new head Coach brings to our lives. Yet how we respond to Him will make our new Coach feel welcome or not. Here's how to make Him feel welcome.

Make a decisive break. I had a pastor friend who left a 12-year pastorate to be the leader of another church. He was convinced this was God's will for his life, but it was difficult to bond with his new congregation. Why? Because he grieved the loss of his previous congregation—so much so that the new church wondered if he was sorry he accepted their call.

Sometimes Christians almost appear to be sorry they became believers. In retrospect the "old life" may look much better than it really was. We act like the Israelites who left Egypt. When things didn't go the way they expected, they began to say, "We remember the fish which we ate freely in Egypt, the cucumbers, the melons, the leeks, the onions, and the garlic; but now our whole being is dried up; there is nothing at all except this manna before our eyes!" (Num. 11:5-6). They failed to remember the slavery, the hard labor and the degradation. They had a selective memory. All they recalled were what they considered to be the "good" things.

In the same way, we remember the friends, the activities that seemed like fun and the temporary pleasures of loose living. We forget the pain, the nausea, the emptiness, the loneliness and the disappointments before we received Christ.

If we want the Coach to feel welcome, we must put any thought of going back to the old coach out of our minds. We've made a commitment, we know it's the right decision, so let's move forward.

Don't linger over vain regrets. For people who came to know Christ at a later age, it's a temptation to wonder what it would have been like if they had trusted Christ sooner. They look at their children, who were raised in a non-Christian home without the influence of biblical teaching. There is no opportunity now to go back and give them what they missed. Often older converts wrestle with guilt because they feel they have failed their family.

As difficult as it might be, we have to put such feelings aside. All the wishing in the world won't change the past, but we can change the future. God promises, "So I will restore to you the years that the swarming locust has eaten, the crawling locust, the consuming locust, and the chewing locust, my great army which I sent among you" (Joel 2:25). Instead of getting bogged down in regret over something you can't change, accept God's promise and trust Him to fulfill it.

If it's too late to be an influence on your children, why not turn your attention to your grandchildren? Live a life that will prove to your family that you are different. Pray that God will allow you, even at this point in your life, to be the witness you should have been years ago. In many ways, grandchildren are God's second chance for older converts to Christ.

Don't be in bondage to past events. There is also no value in dwelling on the events that took place during the years Satan was your head coach. We all have something in our past we wish we could do over. What we must do is confess our sins and claim God's forgiveness. Dwelling on past failure is like living in a graveyard. There's nothing there for us. We have to move on.

That is not to say, however, that we should just forget our wrongs. Wherever possible, we need to make restitution for what we've done. It may mean paying for something you've taken, apologizing for something you've said or taking responsibility for something you've done.

A friend of mine worked in a grocery store during his college years. One of the store's promotions offered free prints of famous paintings. Customers also could purchase a frame to go with it. As the promotion was winding down, the store owner offered the employees their choice of pictures. My friend, however, not only took several pictures, he also took the frames to go with them. Other employees did this, so he thought little about it.

Several years later, while my friend was listening to his pastor preach on stealing, the Holy Spirit impressed upon him that he had stolen the frames. The young man wrestled with his feelings. It was easy to rationalize—he was in graduate school and had little money, he no longer worked for this employer, he didn't even live in that town anymore. Besides, the frames were really cheap—who would really care? But the Spirit gave him no rest. It was clear he had to confess to his old employer and offer to pay for the frames. He made a special trip to where he used to work, met with the store owner and made restitution for his wrong. The man could barely contain his surprise and even offered to take less than what was being given. My friend assured him that this was something he had to do. Later he commented, "I felt like a burden had rolled off my shoulders."

Once we have confessed our sins and made restitution, however, let it be over. Satan loves to come back and say, "Don't you remember what you did? How can you claim to be a Christian with that sin in your past?" Our reply should be, "Yes, I remember. I also remember that Christ has forgiven me. I've done what I can to make restitution and it's over. It's history."

Take comfort in others. The Christians in Paul's day were no different than we are today. They were anything but lily-white. Paul says, "Neither fornicators, nor idolaters, nor adulterers, nor homosexuals, nor sodomites, nor thieves, nor covetous, nor drunkards, nor revilers, nor extortioners will inherit the kingdom of God. *And such were some of you*" (1 Cor. 6:9-11, italics mine). Some of these folks were guilty of the lowest kinds of sin. In verse 11, however, Paul goes on to say, "But you were washed, but you were sanctified, but you were justified in the name of the Lord Jesus and by the Spirit of our God." These Corinthians didn't let their past sins keep them from being used of God, and neither should you. They welcomed their new Coach into their heart, and He welcomed them into His work. That's what you should do too.

John Newton, author of the well-known hymn "Amazing Grace," was also a man with a dark past. He had been rebellious as a youth and insubordinate as a young sailor. Finally, he became a slave trader and gave himself over to the lusts of the flesh. But after God got hold of him and made him a new creature in Christ, Newton became a great preacher and evangelist, as well as a hymn writer. Newton knew how amazing God's grace was; he had experienced it.

Take comfort in the fact that you are not the first to face a shameful past, and you won't be the last. But the past is past. Jesus is now working on your present, and He has great plans for your future. Rejoice in that.

Work with the new system

Have you ever wondered why so many Christians live like non-Christians? Often it's because they are still playing the game by the old rules. They are still using the game plan that Satan laid out for them when he was their coach. If the Lord is going to use you to win people to Him and to serve Him in other ways, you need to:

Learn how to run the new plays. A lot of coaching today has gone high-tech. Instead of chalk and blackboards, many college and professional coaches use computer simulation. They input their game plan into the computer and show their players how it should be executed. In some ways our mind is like a computer. A computer needs to be programmed. For years our old head coach programmed us with untruths. He used television, magazines, friends and even our misconceptions to fill our minds with ideas and methodologies that are contrary to God's will.

Furthermore, information placed on a computer is not as easy to get rid of as it might seem. When something is deleted from a computer disk, it looks like it's gone, but it's not. We can't see it anymore, but it's still there. Numerous programs have been created that will restore the material we thought was lost forever. The only way we can truly destroy the old data is to overwrite it—to write new material over the old information, causing it to be irretrievable.

When we receive Christ, all the old game plans that Satan put into our minds may seem to disappear but, like a computer disk, they are still there. When a crisis occurs or a decision needs to be made, the old game plans resurface and assert themselves. Instead of responding with God's programming, we fall back on what we are most familiar with—Satan's game plan.

The only solution is to overwrite Satan's tactics with the plan our new Coach has given us. That means we need to learn how the Coach, God's Holy Spirit, wants us to play the game. The new Coach's plan has to be studied, imbibed and learned so thoroughly that it wipes out Satan's game plan. Paul has this in mind when he commands "that you *put off*, concerning your former conduct, the old man which grows corrupt according to the deceitful lusts, and be renewed in the spirit of your mind and that you *put on* the new man which was created according to God, in true right-eousness and holiness" (Eph. 4:22-24, italics mine).

Spend time in the playbook. To accomplish this we need to spend time in God's playbook, the Bible. It contains all the strategies we need to play life's game God's way and win. But we must read it, study it, meditate on it, listen to it as it is preached and memorize it if we are going to win.

Unfortunately, most Christians fall drastically short when it comes to knowing God's Word. Dallas Theological Seminary professor Howard Hendricks observes that there is an "almost indescribable ignorance concerning Scripture and theology."[1] James Montgomery Boice, senior pastor at Philadelphia Tenth Presbyterian Church in Philadelphia, claims that the situation has worsened over the past 30 years. He says, "When I came to Tenth, the level of knowledge was higher than it is today—in spite of all my years of teaching. When I preach, I can't assume much prior knowledge of the Bible."[2] Ralph Snowden, an evangelical pastor in north Alabama, says of Christians, "They are less knowledgeable, and more importantly, they take it less seriously."[3] We're like the little boy who was asked if he had any pets. "Well," he replied, "I did have some goldfish, but some water softener got into the aquarium and they softened to death." Because we have failed to master God's Word, we have become softened to the point that we are easy prey to temptation and sin.

This is even more serious because I have never known the Lord to use someone to serve Him who was so undisciplined that he was woefully unfamiliar with the plays in

God's playbook. Bobby Knight, the well-known and some-times controversial basketball coach for the Indiana Hoosiers, demands discipline. He says,

> Discipline is doing what needs to be done,
>
> doing it when it needs to be done,
>
> doing it the best it can ever be done, and
>
> doing it that way every time you do it.

If basketball can make such demands on those who play it, how much more should we be disciplined to deal with the eternal concerns of our soul? If we are going to belong to the team, we have to accept the discipline that makes the team a winner.

Obey the head Coach

There comes a point when we have to decide which head coach we are going to obey. Even though our old nature is dead, we have strong habits built up during the years we were coached by Satan. The devil is a marvelous teacher, and the things he teaches appeal to our flesh. We have learned his plays well, but we need to set them aside. John G. Mitchell correctly observed, "The key to useful-ness, to revelation, and to a Holy Spirit-filled life is obedi-ence to the Word of God." If you want to ensure obedience in your life, you must:

Choose your plays carefully

Ephesians 4:30 says, "Do not grieve the Holy Spirit of God, by whom you were sealed for the day of redemption." I can't think of anything that would grieve a coach more than if, in the middle of a game, his players reverted to the plays taught by the previous coach. It would be a slap in the face. It would demonstrate a lack of confidence in the wisdom of the new coach. It also would be the fastest way to lose the game.

So the apostle Paul says, "Let all bitterness, wrath, anger, clamor, and evil speaking be put away from you, with all malice" (v. 31). Those were the old rules. If someone hurt you, you became bitter or angry. You spoke evil of them and rejoiced to see them hurt. That was how Satan taught you to play the game of life. But the new Coach has a different game plan. He says, "Be kind to one another, tenderhearted, forgiving one another, just as God in Christ forgave you" (v. 32). How much better is the Holy Spirit's plan when compared with Satan's! Instead of bringing hurt, our Coach wants us to bring healing through forgiveness.

In the midst of a crisis, we often choose to react the way we are most accustomed to responding. For many people that means following the old game plan. Therefore, plan ahead. Decide ahead of time the choices you will make if a certain situation arises—and make sure that choice is based on the new playbook. If you can't obey the Coach, you may find yourself sitting on the bench. Jesus said, "If anyone does not abide in Me, he is cast out as a branch and is withered; and they gather them and throw them into the fire, and they are burned" (John 15:6). This is not to say that we lose our salvation, but we certainly lose our usefulness and we miss the rewards we otherwise would have gained. Disobedience always carries a high price.

Confess your sins

Even when we know the plays, we don't always execute them well. Perhaps we tell someone the truth, but we do it in an unloving way. Maybe we see a brother sinning and remain silent, thinking, *I don't want to offend him*, when in reality we are afraid of confronting him. These actions "quench the Spirit" (1 Thess. 5:19). Like all other sins, they inhibit the Spirit's opportunity to use us. They stifle His work in us as well as through us.

The only solution is to confess and forsake those things that hinder the Spirit's work through our lives. In confession, someone has said, we open our lives to the healing, reconciling, restoring, uplifting grace of Him who loves us in spite of what we are.

None of us ever should think ourselves beyond this need. In a painfully honest look at his own life, W. E. Sangster, a well-known pastor and author, made the following observations in his journal:

I am irritable and easily put out.

I am impatient with my wife and children.

I am deceitful in that I often express private annoyance when a caller is announced and simulate pleasure when I actually greet them.

From an examination of my heart, I conclude that most of my study has been crudely ambitious; that I wanted degrees more than knowledge and praise rather than equipment for service.

Even in my preaching I fear that I am more often wondering what the people think of me, than what they think about my Lord and His Word.

I have long felt in a vague way that something was hindering the effectiveness of my ministry, and I must conclude that the "something" is my failure in living the truly Christian life.

I am driven in pain to conclude that the girl who has lived as a maid in my house for more than three years has not felt drawn to the Christian life because of me.

I find slight envies in my heart at the greater success of other young ministers. I seem to match myself with them in thought and am vaguely jealous when they attract more notice than I do.[4]

That kind of honesty is difficult, but anyone who is willing to be transparent before God and confess personal sin will find the Holy Spirit able to use him in extraordinary ways.

Tap into the Coach's resources

Head coaches are not there simply to make a lot of money; they are on the job to teach, to mentor and to give their strength to the players. Furthermore, they are there to tell their players what they are doing wrong, to show them how to do it right and to encourage them. In short, they are there to involve their lives with their players'.

When we belong to God's family, this is what He does for us. Paul says, "My speech and my preaching were not with persuasive words of human wisdom, but in demonstration of the Spirit and of power" (1 Cor. 2:4). Paul had tapped into the power of the new head Coach. The same can be true for you.

In his book *Spiritual Stamina*, Stuart Briscoe tells the story of a man who bought a new computer. Bringing his new possession home, he carefully opened the box, cautiously took the machine out, studied its manual and connected the wires. Eagerly he flipped on the power switch—but nothing happened. Puzzled, the man switched the computer off and rechecked all the connections. He found a screwdriver and fastened the wires more securely. He read again the relevant portion of the manual. Satisfied that he had followed the directions, he flipped the computer on—and again nothing happened. As his frustration rose the man's little daughter walked into the room. "Hi, Daddy!" her cheery voice rang out. "What a pretty computer! Can I plug it in?"

No matter how prepared we are, without the Spirit's power we are bound to fail. Even when we belong to the team, we can play the game only if we tap into our Coach's power.

Now let's play

The next time you watch your favorite team, you may be aware that it's under new leadership. Perhaps a new head coach has taken over and a lot of things have changed. You may see the players struggling with a new system and new plays. When you see that happen, let it remind you that you, too, played on a team, perhaps for 30 or 40 or 50 years, under an old head coach. But now he's gone and a new Coach is on the scene. You belong to a new team. You have to start all over, memorizing new plays and learning new ways. You have to live under a new authority, yet at the same time benefiting from the power of a new leadership. It's challenging! Yet it's also wonderful! The old coach is dead—let's give our lives to serve the new Coach.

---

[1] J. Stephen Lang, "Read Any Good Book Lately?," *Moody*, June 1995, p. 19.

[2] Ibid, pp. 19-20.

[3] Ibid, p. 20.

[4] Gordon MacDonald, *Restoring Your Spiritual Passions* (Nashville, Tenn.: Thomas Nelson Publishers, 1986) pp. 49-50.

Chapter 12

Belonging: New Strategies for Living

Now that we belong to God, He is at work in our lives. Paul tells the Philippians, "Being confident of this very thing, that He who has begun a good work in you will complete it until the day of Jesus Christ" (1:6). But that doesn't mean we can sit back and "go with the flow." As Christians, we still struggle with the problem of sin.

This is not a problem caused by the "old man," who was the unregenerate person we were in the flesh. That man no longer exists; he died at Calvary, and Paul asks, "How shall we who died to sin live any longer in it?" (Romans 6:2).

It's also not a problem caused by the "new man." This man was created by God and does not sin (1 John 5:18). Again, Paul says, "I delight in the law of God according to the inward man" (Rom. 7:22).

So where does this sin problem come from? It comes from the "flesh." The flesh—heart, mind, body—is the trapdoor Satan uses to put his fly in our ointment. It is those habits and responses we learned while under the control of Satan. It is the earthy part of man that has not yet been fully redeemed.

Yet God calls us to holiness. Peter says, "But as He who called you is holy, you also be holy in all your conduct, because it is written, 'Be holy, for I am holy'" (1 Pet. 1:15-16). How can we be holy when we keep committing sins?

Recognize that the normal Christian life is not the cycle of sin—repentance—sin—repentance. Sin is avoidable. There is a part that God plays: He gives us the Holy Spirit, who helps us resist sin. But Christians have their responsibilities too. God's Word gives us some very practical advice on how to avoid sin.

Be careful where you get your advice

Everyone wants to give advice these days. Nearly every magazine has a column with advice on how to do everything from removing spots from your tablecloth to making $100,000 a year working part-time. With the overabundance of advice, it's very important that we are confident of our source.

The psalmist tells us, "Blessed is the man who walks not in the counsel of the ungodly" (Ps. 1:1). When he speaks of the "ungodly," the psalmist does not necessarily mean bank robbers, rapists or drug pushers. He simply means those in whose lives God is not present. If He is not present in their lives, He is not present in their thinking or their advice. When they offer a suggestion, what God wants is not considered. When they suggest a place to go, God's "places" are not on their list. It is also possible for Christians to give "ungodly" advice. When we fail to seek God's mind on a matter through prayer and His Word, we are acting in a purely human vein with purely human wisdom, and what is purely human is ungodly (i.e., without God).

When seeking advice, find a Christian who can help you. Being a Christian doesn't suddenly make you brilliant, but it does give you the mind of Christ (1 Cor. 2:16). Insight from God is better than brilliance any day.

You might object and say, "But I don't know any Christians who are knowledgeable on the subject I'm concerned with." If that is true, begin to search for one who is. Ask around. Seek out others in your church who may be able to direct you to someone. If you are unsuccessful at finding a Christian who can help, then seek the advice of a non-Christian, but always check that advice against God's Word. Does this advice conflict in any way with what God says? Pray about it. Does the Holy Spirit give you peace about it? Consult with other mature and godly Christians. Do they see any way this would dishonor or be disobedient to the Lord? Check with your pastor. What does he think? It's not that God cannot express His will through non-Christians (some biblical examples are Balaam and Cyrus), but you have to be careful when considering their advice. Always make the infallible Scriptures your final authority.

Be careful where you stand

The psalmist continues to describe the blessing of good advice in Psalm 1:1 when he says, "nor stands in the path of sinners." The path that sinners take does not lead anywhere a Christian should desire to go. In effect the psalmist says, "Don't even be found standing there." If you stand long enough in a path used by sinners, you will meet a sinner who will want to take you with him. Solomon says, "I perceived among the youths, a young man devoid of understanding, passing along the street near her [the seductress'] corner; and he took the path to her house" (Prov. 7:7–8). The moral of this story is that since he "just happened" to be near, he was ensnared. How easy it would have been simply to avoid being where the seductress passed by. Solomon continues, "And there a woman met him, with the attire of a harlot, and a crafty heart" (v. 10). While we must hold the woman responsible for her behavior, we must never forget that this young man's problems began because he chose a path he should not have been on. If you follow bear tracks, you dramatically increase your chances of meeting a bear. If you stand in the path of sinners, there's almost no chance you will avoid meeting a sinner.

Teenagers sometimes get frustrated with their parents because mom or dad won't let them "go there" or "do that." They cry, "I'm not going to do anything wrong. You just don't trust me!" What they don't realize is that you don't have to *do* anything to get in trouble. Just by standing on the wrong path you can get run over.

Several years ago I had some friends whose son had a difficult time learning that lesson. Jerry was a good kid, but he had friends who weren't. One day they stopped by to pick him up to go riding. A short time later they were stopped by the police, who searched them and found a stolen CB radio in their possession. Jerry hadn't known about the radio, but he was booked along with the rest for possession of stolen property. On another occasion he was invited to a party. He got there just in time to get "busted" with all the rest for drugs. Jerry didn't use drugs, but he was standing on the wrong path. It took several visits to court, probation and a few other hard knocks for him to learn that it's more than what you do that counts— it's also where you hang out.

If you have a weakness that needs to be curbed, be careful where you stand. Don't go near an adult bookstore; don't go near the racetrack; don't go near a tavern; don't go in your neighbor's house. Take your stand as far away from these places as you can. Where you stand makes a difference in whether you fall. Remember Paul's sound advice to young Timothy, "Flee also youthful lusts; but pursue righteousness, faith, love, peace with those who call on the Lord out of a pure heart" (2 Tim. 2:22). What does this mean? Simply put: if sin is there, get out of there!

Make a convenant with your eyes

This is especially important for men, because men are more visually oriented than women. What they allow to come in the "the eye gate," as John Bunyan put it, significantly impacts them. This is especially true regarding sexuality. Even in his senior years, Job was so concerned about this in his own life that he said, "I have made a covenant with my eyes; why then should I look upon a young woman?" (Job 31:1). Sexual immorality begins with an inappropriate look and deteriorates from there.

The story is told of one renowned seminary professor in his seventies walking down a city street with a young student. As an attractive, perfumed and well-groomed lady passed by the two men, the seminary student did the characteristic masculine double take. Then, realizing his esteemed professor did not bat an eye or acknowledge she was there, the student asked, "Sir, do you finally reach a point in your Christian life where you are no longer enticed or have problems with lust?" The wise senior professor smiled and answered, "My boy, the flesh never gets better, it just gets deader!"[1] Don't expect age to eliminate lust. Age only gives you more time to practice controlling it. If men make a conscious effort to control their eyes, they will find controlling their thoughts a lot easier. Jesus says, "But I say to you that whoever looks at a woman to lust for her has already committed adultery with her in his heart" (Matt. 5:28).

Wandering eyes damage marriages. Wives can tell when their husbands have their eyes on someone else— and it hurts. They can't help but think, *My husband finds this other woman more attractive than me. What's wrong with me?*

We need to seriously consider David Main's advice: "When two people have settled in their minds that 'we are going to love each other,' and they take those vows before God and witnesses, then that puts an end to the practice of comparing. From that day on they are never again to compare. Each is to say, 'The whole of my affection is given to my partner, and I will not allow myself to think romantically about another.'"

Men, make a covenant with your eyes and with God. Where you look can do a lot of harm. The older we get, the more we need to remember that that wife of our youth is the most appropriate person for our affections (Prov. 5:18). In fact, she's probably better than we deserve (Mal. 2:14–15). Let your midlife crisis result in learning to love your wife even more in your senior years.

Crave righteousness

Jesus said, "Blessed are those who hunger and thirst for righteousness, for they shall be filled" (Matt. 5:6). Food and water are the two most vital substances we need to live. They aren't luxuries; they're necessities. Jesus implies that righteousness also is not a matter of choice. It's vital.

Righteousness implies a right relationship with God. We legally receive it when we receive Christ as our Savior. But there is an aspect of our righteousness—our relationship with God—that has to be worked out in practical terms daily. The apostle Paul says, "Therefore, my beloved, as you have always obeyed, not as in my presence only, but now much more in my absence, work out your own salvation with fear and trembling; for it is God who works in you both to will and to do for His good pleasure" (Phil. 2:12-13). Paul is not saying to work *for* your salvation but to work *out* your salvation. In other words, now that you have been made righteous (or saved) through Christ, express that righteousness in the way you live. If your righteousness can't be seen in your life, perhaps you haven't been saved.

Righteous living needs to be our top priority. Jesus said, "Seek *first* the kingdom of God and His righteousness, and all these things shall be added to you" (Matt. 6:33, italics mine). Since we can't enter the kingdom of God without righteousness, we have to seek both together. Jesus illustrates this truth in a parable He told about a king who prepared a wedding feast (Matt. 22:2-13). When those who were first invited made excuses not to come, he said to his servants, "Therefore go into the highways, and as many as you find, invite to the wedding" (v. 9). So they did. But when the king came to mingle with the guests, he spotted a man who was not appropriately dressed for the occasion. The king said, "Friend, how did you come in here without a wedding garment?" The man was speechless. So the king said to his servants, "Bind him hand and foot, take him away, and cast him into outer darkness; there will be weeping and gnashing of teeth" (vv. 12-13). What can we learn from this parable? Simply this: Jesus provides the garment of righteousness, but it's our responsibility to put it on.

You might ask, "How can I hunger and thirst after righteousness?" While Linda and I raised our four children, we noticed that their appetite for good food that their mother fixed was inversely proportional to how much junk food they had eaten before dinner. The same is true in the spiritual realm. Hunger and thirst are natural for living creatures. The process of cells burning calories will create these desires without any effort on our part. If we fill this hunger and thirst with the junk food of the world, we will have no desire for righteousness. Therefore, avoid anything that dulls your appetite for a relationship with God and partake of those things that will nourish it.

Where will we find food that nourishes our relationship with God? Look to His Word. It is not incidental that Scripture calls itself "bread." When tempted with hunger in the wilderness, Jesus answered Satan by saying, "'Man shall not live by bread alone [physical bread], but by every word of God [spiritual bread]'" (Luke 4:4). The Bible also calls itself "milk." Peter reminds us, "As newborn babes, desire the pure milk of the word, that you may grow thereby" (1 Pet. 2:2). It is not surprising that the Bible is also our spiritual "meat." Paul told the immature believers at Corinth, "I fed you with milk and not with solid food [meat]; for until now you were not able to receive it, and even now you are still not able" (1 Cor. 3:2). The Bible is not a book of one-sentence principles to live by. It is not snack food for the spiritually undernourished. It is bread, milk and meat. It is a banquet of high protein, low-fat, essential food. When you hunger and thirst after righteousness, you'll find the Bible to be a tasty meal—a smorgasbord, not a snack.

Let the Spirit control your emotions

A lady once tried to excuse her anger by saying to her pastor, "I blow up and then it's all over." "Yes," her pastor replied, "but have you noticed how much damage an explosion causes?" Negative emotions tend to have negative consequences. That's why Paul says, "Do not grieve the Holy Spirit of God, by whom you were sealed for the day of redemption. Let all bitterness, wrath, anger, clamor, and evil speaking be put away from you, with all malice. And be kind to one another, tenderhearted, forgiving one another, just as God in Christ forgave you" (Eph. 4:30-31).

The solution to embarrassing emotional outbursts is to let God's Spirit take control of your emotions. This may require that you:

Clean out the closets

Often we stuff feelings like bitterness, resentment, jealousy and wrath into the closet of our soul. When someone accidentally opens the door, he is inundated with all that garbage. Ask God's Spirit to reveal to you if there are negative emotions that you have stuffed into your closet and tried to pretend weren't there. Maybe you have bitterness or anger about something that took place years ago. Give God's Spirit the green light to bring it out into the open. Maybe your pastor or a friend can be a listening ear for these hurts. Ask God to forgive you for these sins and bring healing into your life. If you have hurt others because of negative attitudes, ask them to forgive you as well. Your relationship with them will improve immediately, not to mention your relationship with God.

Get God's viewpoint

Hurt, disappointment and anger usually arise because we're looking at situations from a human viewpoint. We forget that God is in control of everything. No one has said anything or done anything that God hasn't permitted for one reason or another. Claim Romans 8:28, which promises, "All things work together for good to those who love God, to those who are the called according to His purpose." Trust that God will use even hurtful situations to eventually bless you. Getting God's perspective will save you a lot of anger, worry and perhaps even a few sleepless nights. If you can trust God for your salvation, can't you trust Him to work out all things for your good and His glory?

Replace the bad with the good

You've heard it said that nature abhors a vacuum. If we simply try to empty ourselves of negative, hurtful emotions, they will only be replaced by something more negative and hurtful. That's why, in Ephesians 4:31, Paul lists the negative emotions we're to get rid of and then immediately continues in verse 32, "And be kind to one another, tenderhearted, forgiving one another, just as God in Christ forgave you." You must fill up that empty place in your heart left by anger and bitterness with the positive emotions of kindness, tenderheartedness and forgiveness. That way, when those other emotions come knocking on your door, you'll be able to hang out a "No Vacancy" sign and be truthful.

Stand against the evil one

After Paul exhorts the Ephesians to put on the whole armor of God, he encourages them three times to stand

(Eph. 6:11, 13, 14). There is a time to flee (as Paul told Timothy) and a time to stand. When Satan sets up a trap to tempt us, that's the time to flee. When we are in the midst of his attack, that's the time to stand. God provides us with spiritual armor that equips us to stand and fight. Therefore, we need to:

Stand against Satan in the public arena

Many of the evils we see in our nation have come because Christians have not taken a stand. When prayer was taken out of schools, where were the Christians? When the Supreme Court handed down its decision in *Roe v. Wade*, where were the Christians? When gay rights legislation was debated and enacted, where were the Christians? Oh, there was a corporal's guard who spoke out against these evils, but the numbers were few. There is enough evil around for each of us to take a stand somewhere. When you have God's mind on the issues He wants you to take a stand on, stand firm. Do not be critical of others who do not stand with you as long as they are standing somewhere else. Choose your battleground carefully.

Prayerfully ask God how He would have you take a public stand against Satan's evil activity. Perhaps God would have you represent Him in an influential public office; perhaps He wants you to speak to your local drugstore about removing pornographic magazines; perhaps He would have you become actively involved in your school system. None of us can do everything, but all of us can do something.

Stand against Satan in the private arena

Satan is as clever as he is evil. He knows which hot buttons to push to make us angry, frustrated or hurt. He has studied our defenses and knows every weakness. When he finds that something achieves what he wants in our lives, he will do it over and over again. The key is to know your hot buttons as well as he does and refuse to respond. Round up all the usual suspects. Plan ahead what you will do when the devil pulls his usual tricks. When he finds out that they don't work anymore, he'll stop trying. Satan is not good at failure.

Someone once said that the person who stands for nothing falls for everything. By taking a stand against the activities of the evil one, you will strengthen your own spiritual life. If you're being tempted right now, do what Jesus did. Tell Satan to hit the road (Matt. 16:23). Put on the full armor of God and take a stand against him (Eph. 6:11). Ask the Spirit of God to strengthen you, for without His strength your stand is like that of a feather to Satan. Remember, "He who is in you is greater than he who is in the world" (1 John 4:4).

Teamwork

Taking the steps necessary to transform our life for the better is actually a team effort. We couldn't begin to think of making the needed changes if it weren't for the presence of God's Spirit. He is the One who makes the essential changes on the inside. We become "new creatures in Christ" (2 Cor. 5:17).

But we also have a role to play in actively cooperating with God's work. If we live carelessly, we can mar the image He wants to create in us, and this will have eternal consequences. When we stand before the Lord and have to give an account of the works we did while on earth, it will be unfortunate if we have not been all that we could have been in Him. While we will not lose our salvation, it will cause us to lose many of our rewards. That's a terrible price to pay for letting fleshly habits have their way.

Native to Brazil is a plant that people call the "matador," or "murderer." It begins by sending out stems along the ground. But once it meets a vigorous tree, the matador attaches itself to the tree and climbs it. As it climbs it sends out arm-like tendrils that continue to grow larger and clasp tighter until finally it strangles the tree. Then from the top, it shoots a huge, flowery head that scatters its seeds to repeat this work of death.

Don't let the flesh strangle your spiritual life. Paul says, "Do not be overcome by evil, but overcome evil with good" (Rom. 12:21).

---

[1] Robert Hicks, *The Masculine Journey* (Colorado Springs, Colo.: NavPress, 1993), p. 69.

Chapter 13

Belonging: The Progress of a Pilgrim

Everything develops in stages. We are born as infants, become toddlers and then develop into young children. From there we pass into our adolescent years. Eventually we become young adults and establish our own homes. Before you know it, we become middle-aged and then move into later adulthood. If the process is not interrupted, we will grow elderly and finally die.

This is normal. No one who is born an infant is expected to stay an infant. While a three-month-old baby belongs to the family just as much as a 30-year-old adult, we do have different levels of expectations for each. We don't blame an infant for acting like a baby, but it would be inappropriate for a 30-year-old to act that way. When understand the stage someone is in, we can adjust our expectations accordingly.

The same is true spiritually. There are different stages of spiritual growth. Some believers are newborn babes in Christ; others are teenagers; still others are mature adults. Regardless of the stage of growth someone is in, he still belongs to God's family. Yet we must adjust our expectations of others, and even of ourselves, according to their level.

There is at least one major difference between the stages of physical growth and the stages of spiritual growth. To pass through the successive stages of physical growth all you must do is stay alive. You don't really have to make an effort—your body will age automatically. Spiritual growth is quite different. While time is a factor, it's not the only factor. Time gives individuals the opportunity to grow, but it doesn't cause it. As Vance Havner used to say, "How long you've been a Christian only tells how long you've been on the road. It doesn't tell how far you've come." Some Christians have been on the road a long time, but they haven't come very far. They are still infants in their spiritual walk.

Because of this, we need to understand the three stages of our spiritual pilgrimage and how to move from one to another.

Stage #1

In Western culture we begin counting a person's age from the day he is born. Other cultures begin before birth. This latter approach considers a child as a human being even though he hasn't been born yet. At this stage a child is severely limited. He can't live apart from his mother's womb. Some body parts can't function until shortly before birth. He has no control over his own destiny. The fetus is vulnerable and, tragically, can die at the choice of a mother, the recommendation of a doctor or the ruling of a court.

There is also something of a prenatal stage in spiritual birth. It's that period before we are born from above by the grace of God. For some people it's a matter of only a few years; for others it may be 20 or 30 or more years. I once led a 91-year-old man to the Lord who had been in this pre-spiritual birth stage for almost a century. Sadly, the majority of people remain in this stage until their physical death. A spiritual birth never takes place. They are never born again. Those in this stage share some characteristics:

They are spiritually dead

We saw earlier that Adam and Eve were made tri-part beings. They had a physical body, a soul (or a life-spark that animated them) and a spirit. Their spirit gave them their ability to communicate and fellowship with God, but it died when they rebelled against Him and ate of the fruit of the tree of the knowledge of good and evil.

All of God's animal creation has bodies and souls, but only man has a spirit. With the death of his spirit, he became little better than the animals he was suppose to subdue. He had lost one of his most important distinctives. Furthermore, this spiritual defect was passed on from generation to generation. Paul says, "Therefore, just as through one man sin entered the world, and death through sin, and thus death spread to all men, because all sinned" (Rom. 5:12).

Man in his natural state is dead in "trespasses and sins" (Eph. 2:1, 5; Col. 2:13). He is born that way. It's like a mother carrying a baby to full term only to learn that the baby is dead in her womb. When the baby is delivered, he is physically stillborn—dead before birth. Likewise, all men and women born since Adam and Eve have been spiritually stillborn—spiritually dead before birth.

Our expectation of dead people should be very limited. It's reasonable to assume that they will only go from bad to worse because that's what happens to a body that has no life. It begins to decompose and return to the natural elements from which it came. Paul warns Timothy, "Evil men and impostors will grow worse and worse, deceiving and being deceived" (2 Tim. 3:13).

We also can expect a dead man to be unresponsive to the things around him. You can place within his grasp the most precious treasures, but there will be no recognition that they are there. Opportunities that would ordinarily be snatched up arouse no interest. Why? Because he is dead. Dead men can't even lift their little finger to God. The same is true spiritually. First Corinthians 2:14 tells us, "But the natural man does not receive the things of the Spirit of God, for they are foolishness to him; nor can he know them, because they are spiritually discerned." God offers men and women treasures beyond value—unconditional love, eternal life, a purposeful life—and they are completely unresponsive to them because they are spiritually lifeless.

They are rebellious against God

But the news is even worse than this. Not only is man unresponsive to the good things of God because he is spiritually dead, but in his spiritual prenatal (or natural) stage, man is an active enemy of God. He is not simply ignorant of God; he is at war with Him. He is dead to good but very much alive to evil.

There is no one who does not believe in a god. Even atheists who deny the existence of God make themselves god. Man's attitude is not a matter of not knowing God; it's a matter of not wanting God. The apostle Paul says,

> For the wrath of God is revealed from heaven against all ungodliness and unrighteousness of men, who suppress the truth in unrighteousness, because what may be known of God is manifest in them, for God has shown it to them. For since the creation of the world His invisible attributes are clearly seen, being understood by the things that are made, even His eternal power and Godhead, so that they are without excuse (Rom. 1:18-20).

God has made sure that no one is ignorant of His existence. The myth of the "innocent savage" is just that—a myth. Whether we're talking about the savage in the jungle or the savage on the sidewalks of Anytown, USA, their hearts are the same. They are rebellious against God.

Paul continues in Romans 1,

> Although they knew God, they did not glorify Him as God, nor were thankful, but became futile in their thoughts, and their foolish hearts were darkened. Professing to be wise, they became fools, and changed the glory of the incorruptible God into an

image made like corruptible man—and birds and four-footed animals and creeping things (vv. 21-23).

They *knew* God; it was not an issue of ignorance. But they wanted to substitute their own gods (they "changed the glory of the incorruptible God"), make up their own rules and live life their own way. Behind every idol is a man who wants to be god.

They are headed for hell

The tragedy for those who remain in Stage #1 is not simply that they waste their earthly life but that they face an eternity separated from God in hell. Many people object to the idea of hell. Robert Ingersoll, a famous lawyer and atheist in the latter part of the 19th century, labeled hell the "scarecrow of religion." He would deliver blistering lectures on hell in which he proclaimed, "The idea of hell was born of revenge and brutality on the one side, and cowardice on the other. I have no respect for any man who preaches it. I dislike this doctrine, I hate it, I despise it, I defy this doctrine!" After one such lecture a man in the audience who was drunk came up to Ingersoll and said, "Bob, I liked your lecture; I liked what you said about hell. But, Bob, I want you to be sure about it, because I'm depending upon you." Those who believe there is no hell had better be sure about their beliefs. The alternative is frightening.

Bertrand Russell, another well-known atheist, commented,

There is one very serious defect . . . in Christ's moral character, and that is that He believed in hell. I do not feel that any person who is really profoundly human can believe in everlasting punishment. . . . I do not think that a person with a proper degree of kindliness in his nature would have put fears and terrors of that sort into the world. . . . I think . . . this doctrine . . . put cruelty into the world and gave the world generations of cruel torture; and the Christ of the Gospels . . . would certainly have to be considered partly responsible for that.[1]

Even some people who call themselves Christians reject the idea of hell. The Church of England issued a document called *The Mystery of Salvation*, which claimed that hell is a state of nothingness rather than a place of eternal suffering. Bishop John Taylor, one of the report's authors, said, "The horrible demons are the imaginations of inventors and medievalists."[2]

But all the sentiments and all the objections don't change the facts. Jesus taught the existence of hell because hell exists. He also taught that it was not originally made for man. In Matthew 25:41 He states, "Then He will also say to those on the left hand, 'Depart from Me, you cursed, into the everlasting fire *prepared for the devil and his angels*'" (italics mine). But since man is guilty of the same offense as Satan (rebellion against God), he will suffer the same consequence.

The good news is that being condemned to spend eternity in hell is not necessary. God never sends anyone to hell. Hell is the natural destination of a freefall from belonging to God. We have a choice. We can rediscover the joy of belonging through faith in Jesus Christ. If we do trust Christ as Savior, we move on to Stage #2.

Stage #2

New Christians

This stage naturally includes those who are new in Christ. They are part of God's family, but they are still learning to obey Him. Everyone has to pass through this stage. For example, I mentioned in chapter 11 that John Newton, author of "Amazing Grace," was involved in the slave trade before he became a Christian. What I didn't mention is that he continued in that trade for several years after he received Christ as Savior—the main difference being that he treated his human cargo more compassionately. Even when he left the slave trade, he saw it as a distasteful but legitimate business. Only later did God open his eyes to the horrors of selling human lives, and Newton became a pastor and zealous spokesman for the outlawing of slavery in the British Empire.

It is true that young Christians need to grow up, but they need the same tender, loving care that young babies deserve. We cannot treat them roughly, unkindly or disdainfully. They can't be expected to have the understanding that comes with Christian maturity. Paul writes in his first letter to the Thessalonians, "But we were gentle among you, just as a nursing mother cherishes her own children" (1 Thess. 2:7). The word *cherishes* comes from the Greek word *trepho*, which means "to bring up, feed or nourish." New Christians need our instruction and encouragement, not our condemnation. They need time and tenderness to grow.

Carnal Christians

Yet others in Stage #2 are what we call carnal Christians. Paul says to the believers at Corinth,

> I, brethren, could not speak to you as to spiritual people but as to carnal, as to babes in Christ. I fed you with milk and not with solid food; for until now you were not able to receive it, and even now you are still not able; for you are still carnal. For where there are envy, strife, and divisions among you, are you not carnal and behaving like mere men? (1 Cor. 3:1-3).

Carnal (the Greek word is *sarx*, which means "flesh") refers to the natural or sensual side of man—his earthly nature.

In Clarksville, Tennessee, the Cumberland Drive Baptist Church stands on a small hill on the bypass around the city. Before the church was built, the area was a dump filled with whiskey bottles, rags, old tires and other trash. At some point the eyesore was covered with dirt and sodded. Then the church was constructed on top of this dubious deposit. Unfortunately, the dump never completely disappeared. From time to time it raises its ugly head. An old tire will pop out here or some rusty tin can there. When that happens, someone has to pick it up and haul it away.

Carnal Christians have the same problem. They are born again, saved from the penalty of their sin, but the garbage from their past keeps popping out. Attitudes and behaviors that they have sodded over but not removed continue to work their way to the surface.

To a certain degree we all struggle with carnality. It is the "body of death" that even Paul had not totally shed and would not until he was removed from his sinful environment and given a glorified body. In Romans 7:14 he admits, "For we know that the law is spiritual, but I am carnal, sold under sin." Like all of us Paul had to say, "For what I am doing, I do not understand. For what I will to do, that I do not practice; but what I hate, that I do" (v. 15).

Yet there is a difference between experiencing carnality and living in carnality. Carnality can pop up in all of us; perhaps it did when Paul refused to take John Mark on his second missionary journey (Acts 15:36-41). Later the apostle reversed his thinking when he told Timothy, "Get Mark and bring him with you, for he is useful to me for ministry" (2 Tim. 4:11). As long as we are alive on this side of heaven, we will struggle with the influence of the flesh. But those who dwell in a state of perpetual immaturity and carnality have a far greater problem.

Carnality interferes with our fellowship with God. He will not participate in our fleshly activities. We must either forsake carnality or forsake God. If we choose carnality, God's Spirit will withdraw into the background and allow us to suffer the consequences of our behavior. We will not lose our salvation, but the divine intimacy that allows us to face our trials and tribulations victoriously will be missing.

Furthermore, carnality is a bad witness. In a carnal condition we say and do things that hurt other people. We bring heartache and grief to our brothers and sisters in Christ. We also cause non-Christians to lose respect for the Christian faith, and we may even become a stumbling block to their salvation.

In addition, deeds done in the flesh create insecurity concerning our salvation. Other people look at us and wonder, *Is he really a Christian?* Satan comes along and says, "If you were really a Christian, you wouldn't be doing this." We begin to wonder if maybe we were insincere when we made our commitment to Christ.

The only way out of this trap is to repent of living as a slave to fleshly desires and move on to Stage #3.

Stage #3

The Christians who occupy Stage #3 are spiritual Christians. They live in an awareness of their daily need for the lordship of Christ. They are spiritually alive and winning the battle against the world, the flesh and the devil. Jesus describes their situation in John 15:5-10:

> I am the vine, you are the branches. He who abides in Me, and I in him, bears much fruit; for without Me you can do nothing. If anyone does not abide in

Me, he is cast out as a branch and is withered; and they gather them and throw them into the fire, and they are burned. If you abide in Me, and My words abide in you, you will ask what you desire, and it shall be done for you. By this My Father is glorified, that you bear much fruit; so you will be My disciples. As the Father loved Me, I also have loved you; abide in My love. If you keep My commandments, you will abide in My love, just as I have kept My Father's commandments and abide in His love.

As Jesus defines them, spiritual Christians are:

Abiding Christians

The word *abide* is used seven times in these verses. It means "to dwell" or "stay put." There is a sense of commitment and permanency. If I tell you I plan to visit you, you might say, "Great!" On the other hand, if I say that I plan to come and abide with you, you may not be as excited. That means I will be moving in with you, lock, stock and barrel, for the duration.

Abiding Christians are committed—there's no turning back. Hernando Cortés landed at Vera Cruz in 1519 to begin his conquest of Mexico with a small force of 700 men. Historians record that he purposely set fire to his fleet of 11 ships. From the shore his men watched their only means of retreat sinking to the bottom of the Gulf of Mexico. With no means of going back, they were forced to move forward into the Mexican interior to meet whatever might come their way.

If we are to abide in Christ, we, too, must destroy any avenue of retreat. We have to burn our bridges. We must let our friends and family know that we have chosen to follow Jesus. We need to invest ourselves and our finances into the cause of Christ (the greater the investment, the less appealing turning back looks). And we need to practice daily surrender to the cause of Christ and our commitment to Jesus as Lord.

Raising your hand during an invitation, saying a short prayer or going forward to the altar are all good responses to your need for salvation. But they have to be followed by more. You must be determined that "this is where I belong and I'm never going back."

Fruitful Christians

Jesus promised that those Christians who abide in Him will be fruitful as well. He said, "He who abides in Me, and I in him, bears much fruit; for without Me you can do nothing" (John 15:5). Scripture talks about at least four types of fruit:

Fruit of character. President Harry Truman used to say, "Fame is a vapor, popularity an accident. Riches take wings; those who cheer today may curse tomorrow. Only one thing endures—character." It is this "one thing" that God is most concerned about. He is intent on building our character even at the expense of our comfort. God's goal, through the Holy Spirit, is to create a character that reflects the nature of His Son. That is why we read in Galatians 5:22–23, "But the fruit of the Spirit is love, joy, peace, longsuffering, kindness, goodness, faithfulness, gentleness, self-control. Against such there is no law." Some suggest that the actual fruit (note the singular) of the Spirit is love, out of which flows joy, peace, longsuffering and all the other characteristics just mentioned. This is certainly a possibility, since "God is love" (1 John 4:8, 16). We know for sure, however, that the mark of a mature Christian character is not more knowledge but more love.

Fruit of good deeds. In Paul's letter to the Romans he mentions a collection taken by the Gentile Christians in Macedonia and Achaia for the poor among the saints who were in Jerusalem. He says, "Therefore, when I have performed this [delivered the offering to Jerusalem] and have sealed to them this fruit, I shall go by way of you [the Romans] to Spain" (15:28). Anyone who has a heart overflowing with Jesus will have a life overflowing with deeds of kindness and compassion. Christians have sometimes been accused of being so "heavenly minded that they are no earthly good." Yet when you consider the hospitals, the orphanages, the inner-city missions, the crisis pregnancy centers and many other efforts to reach out to those in difficulty that Christians have founded, that accusation is pretty hollow. We do not earn our salvation by good deeds, but good deeds are a natural product of our salvation.

Fruit of worship. A further product of fruitful Christians is worship. The writer of Hebrews says, "Therefore by Him let us continually offer the sacrifice of praise to God, that is, the fruit of our lips, giving thanks to His name" (13:15). For a fruitful Christian, worship is not just singing in the choir, praying in church or listening to a sermon. It is the result of a heart filled with love and gratitude that continually and irrepressibly bubbles it way to our lips in praise of our Savior. It is as natural as apples growing on an apple tree or pears on a pear tree. We don't have to work it up or pray it down. It is not restricted to Sunday morning—it fills our whole life. The philosopher may seek to know life, but the Christian who cultivates the fruit of worship will know the Life-giver.

Several of the psalms call on God's entire creation to praise Him. A good example is Psalm 148. Read the first few verses of this psalm and you'll be amazed as the psalmist calls the entire universe to worship God through praise. If the inanimate stars, the sun and the moon are called to praise their Creator, shouldn't men and women who have discovered the joy of belonging have a song of praise constantly on our lips?

Glorifying Christians

When Jesus performed a miracle, He always reflected the glory to God the Father. When Jesus healed the paralytic lowered through the roof by his friends, Matthew says, "Now when the multitudes saw it, they marveled and glorified God, who had given such power to men" (9:8). In the city of Nain He raised from the dead a widow's son, and "fear came upon all, and they glorified God, saying, 'A great prophet has risen up among us'; and, 'God has visited His people'" (Luke 7:16). When He healed the woman who was bent over and unable to straighten up, "she was made straight, and glorified God" (13:13). When He healed the ten lepers, one came back "and with a loud voice glorified God" (Luke 17:15). Jesus always pointed the glory back to God the Father.

Mature Christians are more concerned about glorifying God than they are in retaining the glory that belongs only to Him. Jesus said, "By this My Father is glorified, that you bear much fruit; so you will be My disciples" (John 15:8). A Christian may be bearing fruit, but is he rightfully giving the credit to God?

In 1808, just a year before the death of Franz Joseph Haydn, a grand performance of his oratorio *The Creation* took place in Vienna. The composer himself was present, although in such ill health he was confined to a wheelchair. As the orchestra and chorus burst forth with full power into the passage "And there was light," a crescendo of applause broke out. Moved by the response, the elderly musician struggled to his feet. Summoning all his strength, he raised his trembling arms upward, crying, "No! No! Not from me, but from there—from Heaven above comes all!" Exhausted, he had to be taken from the concert hall, but he made his point. God is the one who deserves the glory. Giving it to Him is the mark of a mature Christian.

Obedient Christians

Obedience rubs most people the wrong way. It's not something we take to naturally. In fact, many people look for every opportunity to remove from their lives any need for obedience. I've read that a bride no longer has to say "obey" in the Church of England's new marriage service. This is the first major change in the rite since the Book of Common Prayer was issued in 1662. A church spokesman said that while the word *obey* does not appear in the service, a bride can opt for it "on the clear understanding that she freely undertakes it, that it is at her request, and that she is not doing it because the vicar or her parents have bullied her into doing it."

Obedience is not an option for a Christian; it's a mark of maturity. Furthermore, it's a symbol of love. Jesus said, "He who has My commandments and keeps them, it is he who loves Me. And he who loves Me will be loved by My Father, and I will love him and manifest Myself to him" (John 14:21). Obedience is the only true test of love. As author and pastor John MacArthur says, "Don't throw God the bone of love without the meat of obedience on it."

Mature Christians have learned the importance of obeying the Lord. They know that the One they trust as their Savior also can be trusted as their Master. If you are moving away from spiritual infancy and on to spiritual maturity, one of the first evidences of your movement will be your obedience to Christ. You won't just *say* you will be obedient; you *will be* obedient!

Obedience ties all the other virtues together. As we seek to do God's will and not our own, we will abide in Him in such a way that our lives will be marked by obedience, for His glory and praise.

Keep on growing

Every living thing grows. As it grows, it passes through stages from birth to death. To become hung up on any stage in between is an indication that something is drastically wrong. If you have discovered the joy of belonging to God's family, don't settle for the entry level to the family. Move on in your relationship with your Father. If you are stuck in spiritual infancy, ask the Spirit of God to help you find the discipline to read God's Word with profit each day, to find quality time with God in prayer throughout your day and to serve the Savior through your local church as often as opportunity presents itself. We are all born into God's family as spiritual infants; we have to start somewhere. No one can help being born spiritually immature, but we are responsible for not staying there. Keep on growing!

---

[1] Bertrand Russell, *Why I Am Not a Christian* (New York: Simon and Schuster, 1957), p. 17.

[2] *National and International Religion Report*, January 22, 1996, pp. 7-8.

Conclusion

And the Joy Goes On

A grade school teacher held a contest. She asked her students to describe what they liked best about their fathers. The winning entry read, "I have so much fun with my father that I wish I had known him sooner." Maybe some of you feel that about the joy of belonging to your Heavenly Father. If you had only known what joy and significance could be yours in the family of God, you would have opened your heart to Christ sooner. I can understand that, but take heart. The joy of belonging will go on forever.

God has planted eternity in our souls. Although each of us can look back to a time when we began, none of us can look forward to a time when we will end. There was a time when we were not; there will never be a time when we are not. Everyone will spend their lives forever in either a positive or a negative relationship with God. For those who reject His offer of salvation, it will be a negative relationship, an eternity spent apart from God. Those who want nothing to do with God will get their wish. Jesus said they will be cast into outer darkness, where there will be weeping and gnashing of teeth (Matt. 25:30).

For all who have received Christ, however, ours will be a very positive relationship, an eternity spent as part of God's family. Once we have been adopted, there's no provision for "un-adopting" us. God has a place and a purpose for each one of His children. Jesus said, "In My Father's house are many mansions; if it were not so, I would have told you. I go to prepare a place for you" (John 14:2).

While we do not know everything about heaven and eternity, we know that we will always belong. The loneliness and lack of understanding we have encountered here on earth will be no more. In his book *Talking to My Father*, Ray Stedman tells the story of an old missionary couple who had been working in Africa for years and were returning to New York to retire. They had no pension; their health was broken; they were defeated, discouraged and afraid. They discovered they were booked on the same ship as President Theodore Roosevelt, who was returning from one of his big-game hunting expeditions. No one paid any attention to them, but everyone watched the fanfare that accompanied the president's entourage, with passengers trying to catch a glimpse of the great man.

As the ship moved across the ocean, the old missionary said to his wife, "Something is wrong. We gave all these years in Africa in faithful service to God, and no one cares a thing about us. Here this man comes back from a hunting trip, and everybody makes much over him. Nobody gives two hoots about us."

"Dear, you shouldn't feel that way," his wife said.

"I can't help it; it doesn't seem right."

When the ship docked in New York City, a band was waiting to greet the president. The mayor and other dignitaries were there. Newspapers ran banner headlines about the president's arrival, but no one noticed this missionary couple. They slipped off the ship and found a cheap flat on the East Side, hoping the next day to see what they could do to make a living in the city.

That night the man's spirit broke. He said to his wife, "I can't take this. God is not treating us fairly."

His wife replied, "Why don't you go in the bedroom and tell that to the Lord?"

A short time later he came out from the bedroom, but now his face was radiant. His wife asked, "Dear, what happened?"

"The Lord settled it with me," he said. "I told Him how bitter I was that the president should receive this tremendous homecoming when no one met us as we returned home. And when I finished, it seemed as though the Lord put His hand on my shoulder and simply said, 'Don't worry, My son, you're not home yet!'"

There is a joy in belonging that every believer in the saving power of the Lord Jesus can experience now—but the real joy is still ahead. Hymn writer Eliza E. Hewitt was right: "When we all get to heaven, what a day of rejoicing that will be." That's when we'll really appreciate the joy of belonging!

Back to the Bible is a nonprofit ministry dedicated to Bible teaching, evangelism and edification of Christians worldwide.

If we may assist you in knowing more about Christ and the Christian life, please write to us without obligation.

Back to the Bible
P.O. Box 82808
Lincoln, NE 68501